# *Pause Ponde*

## Kathy M. Irr

*Merry Christmas 2016*

*Kathy*

Husky Trail Press LLC

Copyright © 2017 Kathy M. Irr

kemi24@juno.com
www.kathymirr.com

ISBN 978-1-935258-42-1

Cover and chapter images by Kathy M. Irr

Husky Trail Press LLC
PO Box 705
153 Boston Post Road, #L
East Lyme, CT 06333

Printed in the United States of America.

# Dedication

For my parents,
**John (Jiggs)** and **Bernie**
whose tender voices I heard before I came into the world.
Those same voices have encouraged, loved,
and supported me throughout my life.
I will love you forever.


Providence decided that I must be patient
in receiving my daughters, and so,
in one blessed year God gave me
two precious women who bring
so much happiness to my sons.
Thank you
**Stefanie** and **Regina**
for your love and friendship.
You have brought us
abundant joy.

'God writes the Gospel not in the Bible alone, but also on trees' -Martin Luther

# Contents

# May

# June

# July

# August

# September

# October

# November

# December

# Introduction

The reflections in this book are a starting place for your own reflection and prayer. Often, my personal experiences are the springboard for these reflections. Some reflections are my thoughts about a story, word, or image that hangs around in my head percolating and wants expression. There are reflections that come out of my personal prayer and desire to connect more intimately with God. There are six opportunities to pause and reflect on the meaning of the words within each reflection. Given the present experiences in your day-to-day life, you may apply the themes in these reflections to your own circumstances.

*The Quote.* Every reflection begins with a quote that speaks to the theme of the reflection. Take time to let the words sink in to your mind and body. Focus less on my intention, and more about your own. How do these words resonate within you, especially given your unique life experiences?

*The Title.* Here's an opportunity to imagine what you might have to say. Given the title of the reflection, what would your short story reveal? It's amazing how a few short words can spark something deep within us.

*Pause and Reflect.* These are my thoughts, stories, and prayers. However, my intention is that it becomes all about your thoughts, stories, and prayers. Is there an idea, a word, or phrase that resonates within you as you pause and reflect on them? Let's face it - sometimes we are reading and we are easily distracted. Our minds wander to our to-do lists, family, work, and daily activities. As we take time to read the words, we want to take time to check in, and begin to feel where those words are hitting home deep within us.

*Ponder.* Ask yourself: is there a message I need to hear, a personal story coming forward, a word I can connect with and carry into my day? Is there another question that arises within me? How do I carry this question inside my body? Don't rush. This is personal time between you and God. Allow God's tenderness to reach deep inside. Let the quiet whisper be heard! God speaks to us in many ways and at different times throughout the day. If something doesn't immediately resonate, it's perfectly OK. Perhaps as you go about your daily activities, something may begin to move forward into your consciousness that calls you to pay attention.

*Pray.* You are given a short prayer to take into your heart and upon your lips should you need one for your day. You may hear yourself formulating your own simple prayer. Take your prayer forward into your day. Gently let the words come to you, especially in those moments when you could use a gentle pause in your day.

*Scripture.* You don't need to take my word. Listen to scripture:
"All Scripture is God-breathed." *2 Timothy 3:16*
"The word of our God endures forever." *Isaiah 40:8*
"For the word of God is alive and active." *Hebrews 4:12*
"The unfolding of your words gives light." *Psalm 119:130*
"Hold firmly to the Word of life." *Philippians 2:16*
"Man shall not live by bread alone, but on every word that comes from the mouth of God. *Matthew 4:4*

Scripture, even when read in small bites, can give us our daily sustenance. God connects with us through the holy words of scripture. We may find joy, reassurance, hope, and food for thought in a simple line of scripture. You may find in time, like I have, that I want more. I read stories and psalms, proverbs and revelations, gospels and songs. Each one reveals not only a little more about our ancestors' relationship with God, but more of our own.

I use three bibles when I sit to read scripture. Each one gives me a slightly different look into the stories and their meanings. I use a more traditional bible such as the *King James* version. *The Life Recovery Bible* offers a Twelve Step recovery overview of scripture. Lastly, I use *The Message* by Eugene Peterson, which is a Catholic/Ecumenical edition written in more contemporary language. Certainly, three bibles are not necessary for applying the simple passages, but, if you find yourself wanting to know more about the scripture passages listed in this book, there are many resources available both online and in the library.

Several years ago, as I began to go deeper in examining my spiritual life, books by several authors helped to give me a place to begin. Little nuggets of wisdom helped inspire new thoughts and possibilities for improving my conscious connection with God. As time went on, and, inspired by those authors, I began to write down my own thoughts and stories. My hope is that with this book you, too, will take the time to let your stories unfold and it will take you into a new or deeper encounter with God.

Take it slow. My intention is not for the book to be read cover to cover in one huge bite. Spend time with a reflection. Allow time for God to reveal your story. You may find it rewarding to journal with your thoughts, feelings, and reactions to each reflection. If something you are reading resonates within you, take it to prayer. Simply talk with God and then listen deep within for God's response to you.

I continue to write weekly reflections on my webpage: KathyMIrr.com.

Blessings as you journey,

*Kathy M. Irr*

# January

# A New Year To Spread Your Tent

*"For last year's words belong to last year's language*
*and next year's words await another voice."*
T.S. Eliot

***Pause and Reflect:*** Listen, friends: we are less different from one another than we may think. We come with our own pasts filled with poor choices, losses, things we feel ashamed of, and tears we've cried over broken promises and unfulfilled dreams. We've had our share of successes and failures, good relationships as well as difficult ones. Some of our choices have been destructive, some have led to much success, and all the while these choices have been leading us toward the persons we are today.

We cannot change the past. Even the minute that just passed is forever unchangeable. So what are we to do with this quickly approaching New Year that can be sustainable? Rather than another meaningless resolution, maybe we can take our cue from Isaiah. "Clear lots of ground for your tents! Make your tents large. Spread out! Think big!…Don't be afraid-you're not going to come up short. You'll forget all about the humiliation of your youth… Your Redeemer is the Holy of Israel, known as God of the whole earth." (Isaiah 54:1-6) Our ancestors certainly learned a few things about surviving in a cruel world.

The image of the tent is beautiful for this New Year. God is asking us to open up our tents-our bodies, minds and spirits- to all the opportunities and possibilities God has in store for us. Don't waste your time with a singular worldly desire; rather open yourself up to something big, possibly unknown. Maybe you've desired a change or shift in attitude, but you're thinking: "it's impossible." With God all things are possible. Maybe what you desire will come to you or maybe God will replace your desire with something greater than what you expected. Don't let your past dictate the future. Don't allow old tapes to hold you back from becoming the person God intends you to become. Allow your failures to fuel your future learning. That's not to say life won't throw us curveballs; that's what life does. This year we can better prepare ourselves to walk through whatever it is life brings our way.

Share your fears with the Holy One and perhaps with someone you trust. The more you bring fears into the light the less power they have to hold you back.

Look to God to restore you to wholeness. Nothing is off limits when you bring God into it. Think big; think conversion. Paul said it best, "...no longer I, but Christ who lives in me." Get ready for one amazing year! God is going to fill you up with what you need. Trust that, and you will find joy and contentment beyond your wildest dreams!

*Ponder:* Look with great anticipation to the New Year. Think really big! Whatever your ideas, creative stirrings, hopes and desires, give them all to the Creator, even your perceived failures and successes. God can have it all. Ask for direction. Let all that you do honor, serve, love, and praise God. Oh, the possibilities!

*Pray:* Dear God, lead me with hope and trust into the New Year. Whatever my hopes and dreams may be, may they be surpassed only by your plans for me. Help me to accept the banquet set before me each day with your grace and blessings.

*Isaiah 43: 18-19*
*Jeremiah 29:11*
*Ecclesiastes 3:11*

# New Beginnings

*"In out-of-the-way places of the heart,
where your thoughts never think to wander,
this beginning has been quietly forming,
waiting until you were ready to emerge."*
John O'Donohue

***Pause and Reflect:*** The new year is an opportunity for new beginnings. So, just where do we begin? Let's start by not complicating things.

More often than not, our approach to the new year is to look at everything we're not doing, and make resolutions that will change things. We may look at our bucket list and see what's missing rather than what's been accomplished.

Here's an idea. Look at all the successes you've experienced over the past year. Notice the areas of your life where personal growth has flourished. What goals have been accomplished and how did you get there? List the gifts that came your way as the result of hard work, mental, physical, or spiritual fitness, or by God's amazing grace. Don't let the strengths go unnoticed and underappreciated. There is a wellspring of wisdom that has no doubt been tapped into this past year.

***Ponder:*** How can you take what you've learned and apply it to your present circumstances? What has been your greatest source of strength? Who has helped you to become a first-rate version of yourself? How has knowledge improved or changed you in any way? How did you respond to answered prayers? Unanswered prayers?

We can make lots of resolutions for the year ahead, but the truth is: everything we need to live a virtuous and fulfilling life is right inside of us.

Start this New Year with a grateful heart. Keep your focus on all the gifts you've received. Let God be in charge of your bucket list. Let the Holy Spirit guide your desires and lead you toward whatever new beginnings are meant to be. Trust whatever has been flourishing in your life, or had its beginnings centered in God, whether you were aware of it or not. Let God continue to lead. Cheers to new beginnings!

*Pray:* Dear God, although we may be unclear about what lies ahead, may we trust in whatever adventure unfurls for us. May we experience your grace and goodness in our everyday experiences, as our continuing story unfolds.

*Lamentations 3:22-24*
*Isaiah 43:18-19*
*Proverbs 16:9*

# Don't Expect Instant Changes

*"Waiting seemed the rawest kind of agony. I wanted God to simply whisk away the masks I had spent most of my life fashioning, to hoist up from my repressed well the lost and neglected parts of myself, to solve my problems, heal my wounds, and alleviate the inexplicable sense of discontent and pain I was feeling. And mind you, I wanted all of this now, immediately, or at the very least soon."*

Sue Monk Kidd

***Pause and Reflect:*** There is no better time of year in New England to talk about waiting than winter. As I gaze from my office window, the ground is icy cold. The trees are barren. The frosty landscape is covered with snow. I'm feeling some resistance transitioning from the Christmas season to the season of the ordinary. Now is the season of waiting.

Ah, but this season can teach us a lot about our spiritual life. There is a lie we often fall prey to, that by waiting, we aren't doing anything with our lives. Waiting somehow makes us lazy. Nothing good can come of us if we aren't being productive.

In the spiritual life our periods of waiting are sacred. For example, the bulb of an iris below the icy surface of the ground is waiting for longer days of light, spring rains and warmer skies to awaken its transition. Its dormant period is as important as the day its petals open to the world.

Sometimes our nurturing process, the stuff going on inside of us, takes a while to produce something beautiful as well. Perhaps we must let ideas toss and turn until we are ready to unleash our creative energy upon them. Sometimes we feel depleted and time seems to be the only healer. There are moments that our impatient mind wants us to rush ahead, and yet, we learn by experience that slowing down, looking at a bigger picture, we are better able to serve those around us and ourselves. When we are full of questions and seem to be at a loss for answers we may have no choice but to ask and patiently wait.

Waiting does not mean we are doing nothing. Actually, it may be that we are actively remaining present to the moment. We are mindful of the indwelling presence of Something Greater than ourselves. We wait for God to answer us in a way we can understand. Sometimes, while it may feel tortuous, just being with the questions is actually the best thing we can be doing.

Our culture of quick fixes and on-demand solutions conflict with the spiritual life. Our spiritual journey cannot be rushed. No amount of our own willpower can change things without God present to them. Life takes us on a magical and mystical ride of its own unique design. We must learn to savor its light and to be present to its darkness as well.

*Ponder:* The next time you feel impatient and want to rush ahead rather than wait:

> want to bury painful feelings rather than accept and bless them and move with God through them,

> think you aren't enough or don't have enough,

> perhaps want to rush the process rather than let it unfold in its proper time,

> have difficulty allowing the questions to just be,

> want answers that can't be answered, *now*, or

> desire to be free and yet remain attached to the drama.

Think about the iris bulb; waiting patiently under the frozen winter ground for the right time to bloom. It *naturally* waits for the promise of spring. Our purpose is simply to rely on God's direction and timing. No matter how many times we try, we cannot force ourselves before we are ready, and expect things to go well. Trusting in God's timing is what faithfulness, mindfulness, and the spiritual journey are all about.

*Pray:* Dear God, teach me to patiently wait on you for answers. Help me to let the process take shape inside of me, and not to rush results that might otherwise not be your desire for me.

*Habakkuk 2:3*
*1 Corinthians 15:58*
*Isaiah 40:31*

# Your Godseed

*"What exactly is a Godseed, and what causes it to germinate? As Christians, we talk about God as being both imminent (present to us, individually and collectively, in our hearts and in our human experience) and transcendent (utterly beyond our reach or imagination, totally 'other' and without limits). My Godseed, I believe, is nothing less than the imminent God at rest in my heart, waiting to be expressed in an act of germination, of resurrection."*

Margaret Silf

***Pause and Reflect:*** I sat several mornings and meditated on the question: what is my Godseed?

For centuries writers have explored the relationship between the universe and our creation. I certainly don't understand a lot about physics, biochemistry, and the like. But this seems clear to me: God never intended for us to live separately from one another or the universe around us. We are interdependent on one another for our very survival.

In fact, scientists tell us that all organic matter was produced in the stars. The same carbon and oxygen atoms and other matter found in the stars are found within our bodies. God, who created the moon, stars, sun, air, and water, formed each one of us uniquely in his image and likeness. Since everything is *of* God, it probably isn't a stretch to believe that we are God's earthly *stars*. Isn't it beautiful to think that we too, have the potential to shine our lights out into the universe? The kind of star power I'm talking about is not ego-centered; rather, it is a sense of connectedness to God, others, and the world around us. Our being here is God's way of saying: I need you in my universe. You are as special as each star hung in space.

I believe that our Godseed is the combination of every beautiful gift our Creator wishes us to possess. It is everything we need to live our lives to the fullest. Our Godseed contains the proper amounts of energy, wisdom, intuitions, feelings, intellect, strength and spiritual fullness necessary to affect the world as God sees fit for us. These gifts contained in the Godseed are to be used for the goodness of humanity and all of God's creation. Our Godseed is unique to each one of us. God knows the time of its planting, the ways it is nurtured, the light it potentially can produce, and the day its light will no longer be seen in the physical world.

***Ponder:*** At the center of our being is a power waiting to be unleashed into the world. In scripture it says, "You would not light a lamp and then put it under a bushel basket." God calls us to open ourselves to the Light, receive it, and give it back out to those who need it. When the light is unleashed in conjunction with God's will for us, it can be transforming. We can then feel a connectedness to the whole of the universe.

Because the universe is infinite and God is as Silf says, "utterly beyond our limits," we can be assured that while our physical bodies return to dust one day, the Godseed that is deeply seeded in our souls will live on in eternity with its Creator.

Spend some time reflecting on your Godseed. What is it? How does it manifest in you?

***Pray:*** Dear God our Creator, help us to care for our interior spaces so that your powerful yet gentle Godseed may germinate and grow within us. May we share the energy of its bloom with others in need of hope, joy, and love.

*Philippians 3:10*
*John 1:1-5*
*2 Corinthians 9:10*

# Deepening The Ties That Bind Us

*"With respect*
*And reverence*
*That the unknown*
*Between us*
*Might flower*
*Into discovery*
*And lead us*
*Beyond*
*The familiar field*
*Blind with the weed*
*Of weariness*
*And the old walls*
*Of habit."*

John O'Donohue

***Pause and Reflect:*** How often do we meet people in our daily life only to stick to the usual script, "Hi, how are you?" or " Where do you work?" or "What do you do?"

How often do we look into the eyes or the heart of a person and wonder about what makes them special? How many times does someone's creativity or gift intrigue you, but you are afraid to pursue a deeper conversation?

Would you feel like it's an intrusion to ask a question that goes beyond the typical superficial exchanges? Fear of the unknown response, fear of feeling foolish, fear of intimacy with others, or fear of rejection are often the reasons we fail to try and penetrate the Christ inside of others. One never knows what possibilities lie ahead when we take a risk in asking another person to share their story with us.

Some of the most wonderful connections and friendships will be made by taking a risk to get to know a person. This may happen either by serendipity or by reconnecting after years. We may want to get to know a person beyond their reputation and judge for ourselves the possibility for a relationship. Perhaps exploring commonalities with another and respecting their differences will give us an opportunity for true friendship.

I remember wanting to ask a high school classmate to play his guitar and sing at a benefit concert the class was sponsoring for a charity. I was the *play it safe* type. He had a reputation as a *wild, dry sense of humor, risk-taker* type. As you might imagine, I let a lot of preconceived notions fill my head. Fears held me back, until one day I decided I would take the risk and ask him to participate in the show. You can probably figure out the rest of the story. It happens to all of us. I discovered a very kind, respectful, and fun-loving young man beneath the reputation. Tapping into his gifts and getting to know the real person forged a lifelong friendship.

Those kinds of relationships are cemented when we are vulnerable, sincere, and honest with another person. When we can accept others as they are, and they, too, take us right where we're at. Gifts that are shared whether through conversation, talents, commonalities, differences, or mutual respect become the thread that leads us to value one another as human beings. There is such great joy in discovering the real stuff of others and not having to twist and turn them to fit our mold. Instead, we begin to interact and learn from one another.

*Ponder:* Take some time to think about why and how your friends became your friends. More than likely along the way you took risks, became vulnerable, and shared parts of your self that went beyond the surface appearance. Undoubtedly, there has been joy and laughter as well as discomfort and trials. Above all, you have loved and respected them for the gift they are to you and others. Your willingness to see their inner Christ, their beams of light, helps them to realize their uniqueness in the world. Seeing Christ in others is not a matter of religion; it is a state of being in love and loving. Take time to quietly thank God for the blessings of friendships in your life.

*Pray:* Dear God, for those still yet undiscovered friendships we ask you for the courage to find the words and deeds that help us go beyond the old walls of habit. Help us to go deeper than appearance, and hold our judgments so that we may discover new relationships based on mutual respect.

*Luke 6:31*
*Ephesians 4:29-32*
*Colossians 3:12-14*

# Spiritual Companioning

*"...the wisdom of spiritual direction*
*is precisely that we refuse*
*to stand between God and the person who*
*so needs to hear God for himself, for herself."*
Gordon T. Smith

***Pause and Reflect:*** What happens at the beginning of a new year? We flood to the gyms to exercise our bodies, begin new diets to get in shape, and take new classes to increase our intellectual capacity or to stir creative juices. There is another avenue we might want to consider when it comes to expanding personal growth. Spiritual direction invites us into a deeper relationship with God. Imagine having an opportunity that leads to more intimacy with God.

The term *spiritual direction* may be confusing to someone unfamiliar with its purpose. It may help to think in terms of spiritual companioning. The purpose of spiritual direction is not to be told what to do or believe. Direction is meant to bring us closer to God. We are invited to set our course in the direction of the Beloved, in a way that helps us to experience God in our daily life.

Spiritual direction provides companionship for our spiritual journey. It's nice to have a workout buddy, a walking partner, or a personal trainer when it comes to our physical health. Losing weight with the help of a support group or coach can make the unbearable more tolerable, and provide long-term accountability. A good teacher makes learning fun and more desirable. So too, with a spiritual director—we are getting support for the soul.

What might a spiritual direction session look like? There are as many variations as there are directors. I will explain my approach, and in general what a person could expect. The director tries to make the meeting space quiet and inviting. We usually speak of *three chairs* in direction: the director's chair, a chair for the person receiving direction, and the vital third chair, which represents God's presence within the session. The session usually lasts about an hour. We meet once a month in the same space. The gifts and blessings of spiritual direction often unfold during the space in time between sessions.

How a direction session proceeds is very much the work of the Holy Spirit.

The person receiving direction may bring questions, issues, concerns, or experiences to share. The director or spiritual companion listens and offers support. Direction is not therapy, although it may feel therapeutic. Advice-giving is not the goal; rather a director may ask a question that helps the person seeking direction to search and listen for the stirrings and movement of God within. Spiritual direction offers the individual a safe and sacred space to begin noticing where God is working in and through their lives.

There is no need to put on airs in spiritual direction. Titles, theological knowledge, education, and faith formation are not necessarily important to the process. One needs only the desire to know God more deeply. And for many people who feel that desire, they still may have no idea how to go about experiencing God's richness in their lives. Sometimes religion has left us feeling edgy; other times we have been drawn to distraction by things that leave us feeling empty. We may have a relationship with God, but desire more awareness or deepening of the feeling of being connected to God.

Your next question may concern the methods used in spiritual direction to help a person enter more deeply into a relationship with God. That too, varies with each director and directee relationship. For example, I offer a process called focusing within my practice of spiritual direction. It helps a person get in touch with their body's responses to everyday experiences. Directors may incorporate prayer, silence, and other techniques to help a person encounter God. Not everyone will respond to a director's style or the process of spiritual direction in the same way. I encourage honesty and evaluation from time to time to ensure the person is receiving what he or she needs from direction and the director.

I've had two directors over the course of many years. Both have had slightly different approaches, and have been a source of great support and hope in my life. They have helped me to better understand the role of prayer in my life and have been sacred listeners through several discernment periods. I've shared my stories and everyday insights with my directors. They in turn have helped to shine a light on how those stories affect my relationships with God and others. They've shared experiences, books, scripture, and questions that have helped me to deepen and expand my spiritual life.

**Ponder:** Spiritual direction is down–to–earth because it is of God. It is right here, in this present moment, where I stand, on this holy ground that I learn more about the God of my understanding. It is in the simple, everyday unfolding of my life that I feel God working in, through and with me. Some days are joyous and free while others feel much more challenging. Whatever the day brings, my desire is to experience God's presence in it. Spiritual direction is one of many ways for me to remain mindful of God's presence in the everydayness of life.

Could you benefit from a spiritual companion in your life? Many retreat centers can connect you with a spiritual director. You may be asked a few questions that will help them find someone suitable for you.

**Pray:** Dear God, give me the courage to seek out spiritual companionship, in whatever ways feel right for me. With guidance and support may I remain faithful to living out your will for me each day.

*Psalm 27:4*
*1 Corinthians 2:13*
*Proverbs 4:7*

# Living Into Our Marriages

*"The most amazing fact about Jesus,*
*unlike almost any other religious founder,*
*is that he found God in disorder and imperfection*
*- and told us that we must do the same*
*or we would never be content on this earth."*
Richard Rohr

***Pause and Reflect:*** Preparing for a presentation on marriage, I came across a very simple yet strikingly encompassing definition of marriage. It is the communion of love and life.

The communion of love is a bringing together of the very intimate thoughts and emotions that we feel, think, and act upon. The communion of life is all our physical, emotional, and spiritual experiences not only from when we met and dated, but also from childhood. Sometimes that *baggage* is light; sometimes it's heavy. The glue that holds it all together is the spiritual life. God helps us to sort through what's really important and what needs to be let go, sustained, or improved upon.

You've probably heard the saying, "my marriage isn't perfect because I'm in it!" There comes a time in most marriages when the communion of love and life is very challenging. Misunderstandings, hurts, changes, and losses can have us pointing fingers at one another. Our need to control, to be right, and to demand understanding can turn grudges into resentments. It's as if two people who once walked side-by-side are drifting further and further into their own self-centered worlds. This happens to really good people.

This is where Christians can look to Jesus as our perfect example. He is Love personified. He walked right into the messiness of life and asked God the Father to be present to him. If we understand marriage as vocation then we, too, are asked to bring God into the messiness of our lives as well. Healing begins when we ask God to be present as we speak and act toward one another with unconditional love. Love is a choice and God wants to help us expand our capacity to love.

For example, we can ask God to help us love our spouse and stop waiting for them to love us as we think we should be loved. We can ask for patience as our love grows and changes. We can invite God into the storms until things settle once again and invite him to stay during the peaceful times too. We can ask God to help us resist always wanting things our way. We can pray to accept the imperfections in our spouse rather than rudely point them out.

*Ponder:* Jesus loved perfectly. We won't love that way, but it's certainly worth every effort we can put forth to try harder. As we commit ourselves to placing God at the center of our lives and letting that love seep out from us into our relationships, we are choosing to deepen and grow our love.

Do people who see you as a married couple see God in your love for one another? How can you choose to love your spouse with more depth today? Think of the choices Jesus made to love. How can you follow his example today?

*Pray:* Dear God, may we bring unconditional love to one another and not let negativity control our lives. May we find kind words and gentle gazes for each other. May we learn to forgive and find the gifts each one brings to the relationship.

*Hosea 2:19*
*Mark 10:9*
*Ephesians 4:2-3*

# February

# Not In Our Time, But God's Time

*"The two hardest tests on the spiritual road
are the patience to wait for the right moment
and the courage not to be disappointed
with what we encounter."*
Paulo Coelho

***Pause and Reflect:*** Let's put some perspective on this virtue we call patience. How often do you feel yourself losing patience in a checkout line, at the store, or doctor's office? Are there unanswered prayers that have you doubting God's presence in certain circumstances? Have you made a decision out of frustration rather than using prayer or discernment to find an answer? How many times have you heard the words cancelled, or postponed, due to weather? These circumstances have fixable solutions. Other circumstances, however, may seem to leave us reeling with emotions for much longer periods of time.

Waiting for outcomes is not easy, especially when we have our own ideas about how we think those outcomes should look and feel. Those who wait on God with integrity and complete trust understand a few *truths*:

*There is a difference in our attitude toward life when we have a God-centered purpose vs. a me-centered purpose.* When we trust God regardless of circumstances, we see more clearly what is important in life. God won't allow us to take people for granted. God's desire for us is to explore all of life's invitations and possibilities. Sometimes there are no short cuts. A heart and mind focused on God is grateful for whatever it is that is deepening inside of us. The person we are becoming is of greater importance than the *things* of life.

*Waiting helps us cherish our God-given gifts.* We appreciate the fruits of our labor when we persevere through challenges. We may not like experiencing difficulty, but in the end, coming through adversity teaches us who God is calling us to become. Patience helps us grow emotionally and spiritually.

*Transformation happens over time through life's trials and joys.* We gain wisdom with every life experience that draws us toward God. The author

Michael Higgins describes the wounds of our past as gateways to a new life. He goes on to say, "these gateways to new life define the terrain, the hills and valleys, contours and lines, of a psychological and emotional life aching into holiness." Do you see your present circumstances as a bridge to new opportunity?

*Wisdom brings us closer to understanding there is a God who loves us unconditionally.* God is in no rush. As our trust and dependence on God increase we begin to understand that the long-term results, those that we may not fully appreciate in the moment, mold us into a finished product with a purpose known and treasured by our Creator.

**Ponder:** Next time you feel yourself rushed or challenged by circumstances, facing adversity, or running low on patience, try these steps: Stop. Get quiet. Ask your body where it is feeling these emotions. Ask God if there is a story within the feelings. Allow it to unfold if possible. If not, simply acknowledge the feelings and ask God to place a comforting light around them. Ask God if there is an opportunity to use this pause as a bridge to a new understanding. Remind yourself that it's not necessary for you to see the whole picture. Today you may receive a small glimpse. Thank God for whatever gifts come from your willingness to be patient and understanding with yourself. Ask yourself these questions once you try this exercise. What did I experience in the exercise? Was there some kind of shift within my body, attitude, or emotion? What will I take away from the experience that may be useful in the future?

**Pray:** Dear God, help me to understand that transformation is happening slowly, one day at a time, so long as I place my trust in you.

*Philippians 1:6*
*Matthew 19:26*
*2 Timothy 3:16*

# Evangelization, Comedians, and Blizzards

*"I am a little pencil in the hand of a writing God
who is sending a love letter to the world."*
Saint Mother Teresa

**Pause and Reflect:** What do evangelizers, comedians, and blizzards have in common? Well, of course, they help to prepare us for leadership. Stay with me.

No one likes hearing our spiritual leaders talking at us. Surely, they are more effective leading us towards God by example. I attended morning mass and the priest gave a homily on evangelization. He was referring to the scripture reading of the day, in which Paul was passing along what he had learned about Jesus to Timothy, a young man trying to provide leadership to a Christian community that was stubborn, self-reliant, and defiant when it came to following God's will.

We can be that way, especially when we focus on external things rather than prayer and spiritual insights. At these times we simply refuse to ask for assistance from God, falsely believing we should have all the answers.

The priest mentioned a conversation he had with a grumpy, hard-hearted man. During the conversation the priest gently confronted the man about his disposition. The man became grumpier. The priest smiled. This seemed to annoy the man even more! The priest again smiled and asked the man to smile with him. The man huffed and puffed and relented, probably thinking he'd rid himself of the persistent priest. He smiled. The priest said nothing and simply walked away. This request to smile changed something inside of the man. Perhaps he thought no one cared whether he was grumpy or not. Later on, he thanked the priest for his message. And what was the message? Love. Attention. Caring. Encouragement. Sincerity. A smile made a difference. Evangelization begins with our smallest and most sincere actions.

I attended a comedy show at a local theater. Midway through the evening I was aware of my facial muscles...they actually were feeling tight from all the laughter. Blessed be the comedians among us who help us to forget our inhibitions.

Author Emily O'Shaughnessy describes how a great comedian keeps the audience engaged. There is no doubt that as evangelists we too must incorporate some of these techniques.

Comedians and evangelists must know their audience. As Paul and Timothy traveled and preached they understood the people to whom they were speaking. Many were struggling with their faith. Paul understood more than anyone what it was like to lack trust in God. The wisdom we share with others often comes from our own personal experiences, both our failures and joys. The comic is quick on his feet and knows the mood of the crowd. So too, we must trust the movement of the Spirit within us when we are given opportunities to share our faith either in words or actions.

Our material must be timely. People want to understand how Jesus' words affect them today. For example, what does it mean when Jesus describes himself as the vine, his Father as the vine grower, us as the branches bearing fruit?

Back in Jesus' time, the vine was an apt visual, as vineyards dotted the landscape. His followers could relate. Today, for example, an oak tree may provide a better visual for a person living in the northeast United States who is explaining the same parable. How can a tiny seed of hope planted within us, help us grow into a sturdy and faithful follower of Jesus? How does one rely on God as a source of strength? Reading scripture may seem meaningless unless we help others connect it to their present circumstances and surroundings.

Timothy was guided by Paul to develop his leadership skills with the people of Ephesus. It took practice, practice, practice. I imagine, like a comedian who practices jokes over and over, those who evangelize must prepare themselves through prayer, meditation, and continued studies. Even when God gives the gift of communication, the message must continually be practiced and lived on a daily basis. Trust is gained through truth and authenticity.

Collaboration is key. A comedian is not successful on his own. He has writers and stagehands, assistants and the audience. All are essential for the message to produce the desired effect. Faithful leadership cannot come from a place of ego-centeredness. It must be focused and centered in God. The most effective spiritual communities have members who work with one another to do the work God is calling them to do. Self-adulation is put aside for the better of the whole.

You must be wondering how blizzards tie into this picture? My friend Greg, a native Alabaman, referred to a recent New England winter as the *Snowpocalypse!* How does a huge storm prepare us for leadership?

Sometimes we need to get away from the routine. When storms come out of seemingly nowhere, we need to assess, prepare, hunker down for the long run and trust God with the big picture. Some people say, "I can't go anywhere!" or "this ruined my plans!" or " what am I doing here?" My response? "Contemplate that."

*Ponder:* Spiritual leadership isn't for the faint of heart. It can be demanding. Coming to know God is a loving and challenging experience. We must allow God's light to shine out from within us. Don't be discouraged, either in your own lack of faith, or someone else's. Remain teachable.

In the end spiritual leadership makes us whole. Our audience is the people we come in contact with every day of our lives. Do your very best to make everyone you meet feel special. We don't have to shout God's name to evangelize; we need only reflect his light to others. Like the comedian, we must have a sense of humor and not take ourselves so seriously. And as with the storms of life, we must learn to move in them with grace. We are all called to evangelize in the name of LOVE and that call comes to each of us in a variety of ways through the Spirit. How have you been called to evangelize in your daily routines? How comfortable are you when it comes to sharing your faith? How have you shown leadership in your faith community?

*Pray:* Dear God, I stand ready to serve you today. Help me to speak and act in a way that reflects my willingness to live out your gospel message of love. Take any discouragement I may feel, and fill me with resilience and determination to continue spreading the Good News.

*1 Timothy 4:7*
*Acts 2:39*
*Romans 10: 12-15*

# A Valentine To Remember

*"Love is not maximum emotion. Love is maximum commitment."*
Sinclair B. Ferguson

**Pause and Reflect:** Spend a little time reflecting on what others have to say about love:

"...it's a blessed thing to love and feel loved in return." E.A. Bucchiarneri

"Tell your heart that the fear of suffering is worse than the suffering itself. And no heart has ever suffered when it goes in search of its dream." Paulo Coelho

"Your task is not to seek for love, but merely to seek and find all the barriers within yourself that you have built against it." Helen Schucman

"A sacrifice to be real must cost, must hurt, and must empty ourselves. Give yourself fully to God. He will use you to accomplish great things on the condition that you believe much more in his love than in your weakness." Mother Teresa

"In this world, it is too common for people to search for someone to lose themselves in. But I am already lost. I will look for someone to find myself in." C. Joy Bell C.

"Many times, when I was having a hard time with one of my children, God would always remind me that He was having a harder time with me than I was with them." Charlie Jones

My understanding of love has grown and deepened over the course of my lifetime. And yet, quite honestly, I still need to remind myself that, first and foremost, I am a beloved child of God, and that's enough. It's easy for me to get caught up in the emotional feelings attached to a joyful experience and to feel God's love present in it. It's much more difficult to feel God's love in the challenging and painful experiences of life and envision a blanket of warmth wrapped around me.

Sometimes God calls me to places and to be with people that are not familiar to me—for example, when I'm asked to do a presentation. My heart quickens and my insides feel uneasy. Will I be accepted? Will they understand my vulnerability? Will I honor God with my presence rather than massage my ego? If I am to continue dreaming and creating, I must let go of anything that holds me back from doing God's will. I must courageously welcome love to fill the spaces fear has carved out inside of me.

Emptying myself of self. Wow! That is not easy, and yet, to let go completely is to recognize that God's power can fill me up and satisfy me completely. I no longer need anyone's approval to feel authentic. Don't get me wrong; people often help us to see who we really are. It feels wonderful to receive and accept a compliment. It's lovely when others appreciate who we are and what we do. However, I can let go of being an approval junkie. The wisdom of the Spirit helps me discern an ego-centered act from a God-centered one, and hopefully, I respond from the latter.

God reminds us that our invitations to tomorrow have not arrived yet. I must remain in the present. God is right in there with me no matter the circumstances. If I put my hope and trust in God, every tomorrow I'm supposed to experience will come in God's appointed time. God's got a handle on it! And that goes for the people in my life. God has them too. The best thing I can do is step out of the way and let God do his work.

***Ponder:*** It may not be Valentine's Day; however, envision receiving a card from God. Perhaps one of these many salutations are awaiting you…

Open Your Heart
Let Me In!
I've Got This!
You and ME, Together Always
First Love
Beloved…Be-Loved

With God, we have an affair of the heart every day. What would God's salutation be to you today?

***Pray:*** Dear God, fill me with your love today. May I receive it with grace and give it away with fervor.

*1 Corinthians 13:7-8*
*Galatians 2:20*
*Philippians 2:2*

# The Hyphen

*"A hyphen can bring you from nowhere to now-here."*
Rana J. M. Gohar

***Pause and Reflect:*** According to Webster's Dictionary, a hyphen is a sign used to join words to indicate they have a combined meaning or implied element.

The open-minded person may welcome the thought of a hyphen as an opportunity to pause. Perhaps it is a point of emphasis when we link words that help us stop and think: there is more here to ponder.

We've all experienced feelings of uncertainty. Gohar suggests that we can bring our thoughts from a place of emptiness or confusion to the present with one small symbol. The emphasis is placed on living in the moment no matter what circumstances seem to burden us in the present. Could the hyphen help us move a little deeper spiritually? Let's look at a few possibilities:

Ever-mindful: I have a friend, who, when she sends an email, uses these words in her closing salutation. It always makes me pause, then smile. Ever-mindful reminds us that there is only one really important question that matters today. What does God ask of me now? Placing God at the center of our being is a way of feeling reassured of a Higher Presence guiding us into the "whatever" moments of our day.

God-like: We are all called to be holy. In Greek, the word perfect, telos, when translated, means goal, end, or purpose. We can ask the question, "What is the purpose for which God has created me?" To be God-like, then, does not involve ego. It's quite the opposite, in fact. Through mature growth we are moving toward becoming the person God intends us to be. The power to be molded and changed comes not from our doing but from God. We are not equating ourselves with God; rather, inching toward holiness, we trust being led in God's direction. Only God is perfect. We seek purpose rather than perfection.

Fine-tune: Just as a member of an orchestra makes small adjustments to his or her instrument in order to achieve the most beautiful sound possible, we too, make small adjustments to our daily experiences in order to better feel God's presence in them. Taking five minutes for prayer or meditation, getting outside in nature, or reflecting on a piece of scripture helps us to fine-tune our relationship with God. A deep breath or pausing for just a minute may give us time to collect our thoughts rather than spewing out words we'll later regret. Listening to our gut, that place where the Holy Spirit resides, may help us find our authentic voice. Making small adjustments can make a large impact on our well-being.

Open-hearted: Freedom! Letting go of our expectations frees us for happiness. Our hearts sing when we throw open the doors of possibility and potential in others and ourselves. We get out of the way and make room for the movements of the Spirit. We do not stifle our feelings and emotions; rather, we find a welcome place within ourselves to acknowledge them. And when aching, loneliness, and suffering test our hearts we pray to accept it with courage and grace. God knows our hearts better than anyone. May our willingness to open our hearts to the Beloved invite endless adventure, while squashing those no longer useful absolutes.

*Ponder:* Spend some time exploring the hyphen, the pause. If you come across a hyphenated word that puts a little more emphasis on your spiritual outlook, take a closer look at its impact. Create hyphenated words that speak your language. Words are just words until you let them penetrate your soul. Let the words tell you your own story. What words need a hyphen? What did you discover about yourself in the pause?

*Pray:* Dear God, create in me a playful spirit. Help me to explore your purpose for me in this day and let whatever I do and say honor you.

*Lamentations 3:40*
*Psalm 77:6*
*Ecclesiastes 2: 24-25*

# Servant's Song

*"No truth is more pervasive in Scripture and Christian tradition than this one- that real freedom is found in obedience and servanthood. And yet no truth is more incongruent with modern culture. Here we stand before a stark either-or: the gospel message of true freedom versus the culture's ideal of self-creation, autonomy, and living 'my way.'"*
Roger E. Olson

***Pause and Reflect:*** Jesus is the model of the humble servant. He has compassion for the weak, injured, lonely, and broken. We may think immediately of the homeless, mentally ill, bed-ridden elderly, abused, and the poor. We are called to serve our brothers and sisters in need of our support.

I sat in an inner city train station for over two hours waiting on the ride that would take me to my comfortable home. It was cold and damp outside. Unable to find an empty bench inside the terminal, I sat against a wall on the floor trying to remain invisible. I watched small children play as drug dealers sold their poison. Homeless men and women with sores covering their bodies found places to rest throughout the station. I noticed a mentally ill man hallucinating and conversing with no one in particular. Some of the people looked hungry. Others looked cold. Sad and distant eyes seemed hopeless and begged for recognition.

Honestly, I felt uncomfortable. There was even a feeling of fear at times. I thought to myself: I do not know the world they live in and yet, I'm a part of it. Several persons caught my attention and I wondered about their lives, their struggles, and their dreams. Questions floated in my head; did they feel loved? Was a nutritious meal awaiting them? Did they have a job? And did they feel safe when they returned home?

I thought about what I offer to humble myself to the service of others. The answer is: not enough. Do I offer my time, talent, and treasure out of a sense of obligation, or from a place of humility? Sadly, there are often strings attached in some way.

This day in the train station, I felt as though I had little to offer. I quietly prayed and asked God to remove any intolerance, judgment, or cynicism. My mind and heart began to soften. The fear melted into awareness. I heard Jesus' voice tenderly whispering to my heart, "don't look away." Instead of turning my gaze, I began to let my eyes meet theirs. I offered a smile when it was appropriate. I recognized each person's dignity and offered a silent prayer of hope; hope for them, and for a world in need of Jesus' compassion.

I've volunteered in soup kitchens, low-income housing, a group home for the mentally ill, camps for children with disabilities, and a women's prison. In these situations, there was a comfort zone. I could always look to someone for support or help if necessary. This experience in the train station was raw. This was reality without many boundaries, and in some ways more challenging than other experiences. It was a personal call to respond without a set of directions previously established.

**Ponder:** We are called to take up the basin and the towel, to find ways to wash the feet of those in need of our love. It's not always how much we can offer, so much as how we offer it. If our intention is to place God at the center of every thought and action, we cannot fail. Once we encounter the holy presence of God, we realize no matter where we are, we stand upon sacred ground. God will challenge us. God has the power to change us. As Paul said in scripture, "…it is no longer I who live, but Christ lives in me." (Galatians 2:20)

**Pray:** Dear God, may I see your face in the lonely, poor, and downtrodden of our world. Fill my heart with your Presence, and my hands and feet with holy desire to do your will. Replace my fear with kindness, my judgment with tolerance, and my resignation with compassion.

*Matthew 6:33*
*Proverbs 22:9*
*Daniel 4:27*

# Seek Peace and Pursue It

*"Peace is always beautiful."*
Walt Whitman

***Pause and Reflect:*** The words, "seek peace and pursue it" written by St. Benedict are a reflection of Psalm 34:13 which says, "Turn from evil and do good; strive for peace with all your heart."

It's difficult to read newspapers or watch TV without becoming distracted by the unrest and violence in our world today. The problems that often cause the unrest seem so overwhelming that we might ask how one person could possibly effect change toward peace? I imagine St. Benedict probably looked out at his world and felt much the same.

Peace comes to us as the result of a loving and centered heart. To seek and pursue peace I must want it for myself. We cannot want peace for others without first seeking within.

We seek peace when we are quiet inside. When we ask God to be present in our decision-making. When we do not let hurtful words spill out in anger, vengeance, or jealousy. We seek peace when we don't insist on being right, when we let little things that don't really matter slide. When our opinions are just that and no more. When competition is not used to embarrass another.

The seeking begins right in our own backyard. We practice peace in our homes, workplaces, schools, and places of worship.

We pursue peace through prayer and action. We cannot just talk about it. We must act justly and fairly. The great equalizer in my mind is not power, money or fame, but rather, respect and love.

***Ponder:*** Hold the words of Saint Benedict in your heart and mind as you move through your day. You may not be able to effect change in the whole world, but you can change your little piece of it. Ask yourself how you experience peace in your body. What can you do to pursue peace in all your affairs today?

*Pray:* Dear God, remind me that everywhere I walk is holy ground. Let me keep a peaceful heart with all those I encounter in this day.

*John 14:27*
*John 16:33*
*Philippians 4:6-7*

# Living Into Prayer

*"The function of prayer is not to influence God,*
*but rather to change the nature of the one who prays."*
Soren Kierkegaard

***Pause and Reflect:*** Is your prayer life stale, lacking or uninspired? Could it be that perhaps old tapes are playing in your head?

Let's look at stripping away all the agendas, the airs we put on, the masks we wear and the shoulds we've placed on ourselves and come to God purely with the purpose of opening ourselves to the Spirit's direction.

Picture yourself in a safe place, take a breath, and let your body and mind relax. Rather than your body being an object of observation, imagine yourself being a vessel open, free, and waiting to be filled. Fold your hands into prayer position or simply open your hands, palms upward, and continue to imagine you are basking in a great warm light. Speak freely, voice your concerns, desires, requests, and questions. Sit quietly and allow whatever is spoken in the silence to resonate within you. Sink into the quiet and take some time. When you are ready, move back into your day with the confidence that God hears you and is present. Focus on living intentionally and remain consciously aware of a Higher Presence. To live intentionally we must direct our words and actions toward thanking, praising, and serving God.

Humor, joy, and laughter are as essential to prayer as is quiet. Praying and playing are necessary to living a holy and balanced life. To be holy is not to be perfect. It is to be real and to strive to be who God is calling us to be. We learn who we are called to be through prayer and discernment.

Prayer is less about how much we say and more about how we live. Praying into our ordinary, mundane, everyday experiences is where we encounter God. We experience God in our morning routine, at our workplaces, in our daily meetings, as we drive, exercise, cook, and clean. We experience God in our homes, churches, nature, and sacred spaces. We experience God in the quiet, in the noise, in our sadness, fear, pain and anxieties as well as our triumphs and happiness. Sometimes the people we bump up against aren't pleasant. And sometimes because of our own stuff or as the result of things we cannot control, we find ourselves in uncomfortable situations. Life doesn't always *feel* good.

*Ponder:* Perhaps a change of perspective will help. Many people tell me they have a difficult time finding God. Could it be as simple as…God is…Rather than finding God we need to experience God and act as if God is…present…listening…aware…interested…compassionate…forgiving…surprising…awesome…Light and Love…God is in the midst of our present circumstances and experiences.

Today, whatever box you've placed God in, surrender it. Let go of old tapes, old habits, past resentments and ideas that have held you back from an intimate relationship with God. Pray simply. Talk to God wherever you are and wherever you're at! Allow yourself to experience the God of surprises!

*Pray:* Dear God, open me up to whatever experiences you wish me to have, whomever you wish for me to encounter, and let me feel your presence in all I do and say this day.

*1 Chronicles 16:11*
*Psalms 5:3*
*1 Corinthians 14:15*

# "...Rather, He Emptied Himself..."

*"The ego hates losing - even to God."*
Richard Rohr

**Pause and Reflect:** Those words, found in Philippians 2:6-7, are a powerful and loving reminder of our need to surrender all things to God. The miracle of surrender is that we no longer have to fight feelings, old patterns, or past truths. We simply let go of preconceived notions. We don't have to be anybody. It's like letting all the air out of a balloon.

Surrender is emptying oneself of the part of self that wants to cling to anything other than God's will for us. It's letting go of the excess, the extra stuff, the baggage of the past, the shoulds. It is trusting that even before the process of emptying begins, God already anticipates our need to be filled.

What we are releasing are all the things that stand in the way of goodness, possibilities, potential and yes, holiness.

We place ourselves in God's hands and go about our day believing that our intuition, reasoning, education, and gut instincts will guide us to make inspired decisions. After all, these are God-given gifts. We are the vessel through which God moves. We do have the choice to receive and act as a conduit or not. To be "the light to the world," as we are called to be, means we must discern when to say yes and when to say no. Both are appropriate responses depending on our circumstances. God desires that we use our gifts, talents, and treasures toward a better world.

Surrender takes awareness, willingness, and above all practice. It's most difficult when we believe we *should* have the answers or when things don't go as we planned. A wise person once commented on success: "It is not how well we execute Plan A, it's how smoothly we cope with Plan B."

The more we empty ourselves, the more we can be filled by a Spirit of goodness and love. And if all our intentions begin with those two things, goodness and love, we will be better people and we will make a better world around us.

*Ponder:* Today, I choose to surrender myself to God's will for me. I will accept the unconditional love dwelling within by listening and paying attention to the movement of the Holy Spirit. What does surrender feel like inside my body? Is it a familiar feeling or is it a new feeling?

*Pray:* Dear God, help me to empty myself of needless worry and distraction that I may focus on your plans for me today.

*Matthew 19: 27-29*
*Mark 8:34-35*
*Philippians 2:5-8*

# March

# Back to the Drawing Board

*"Things don't go wrong and break your heart
so you can become bitter and give up.
They happen to break you down and build you up
so you can be all that you were intended to be."*
Charles Jones

***Pause and Reflect:*** It's almost maddening! Those times when you think you've really worked through an issue or on a relationship only to find yourself back into the muck of feelings and perhaps reacting in an unproductive manner. It's that moment you find yourself asking, "How did I get back here ...AGAIN???!!" Sometimes, it's tricky trying to figure out what we can change and what needs to be let go.

These steps help us to remember that we are not alone in dealing with the twisted and sometimes unfair or yucky things that happen in life. The key is commitment to practicing them:

*Admit there is a problem.* Saying, "I don't care," or, "It doesn't bother me," or, "It's not my problem," when clearly I'm affected by it, really does me no good. I need to own my feelings. Honesty about what is causing me to feel out of sorts is the only way to begin dealing with the problem. Allowing myself to feel the feelings without judgment is a good place to begin.

*Admit my part in the problem.* How has my behavior contributed to the situation? It's easy to look at the person or persons on the other side and begin listing off their indiscretions; however, it's important to focus on any changes that I can make to help to rectify the situation. My job is not to change them. Leave that work to God. Be careful at this point. It's easy to say, "I've searched myself and I did nothing to provoke this." This may be true; however, you are still holding on to it, so there is something more to consider, and quite possibly to surrender.

*Ask God for help.* This is the place where a lot of us get stuck. It's not that we don't believe in God; we just don't think we need to bother God with it. We think we should be able to handle this on our own or may not feel deserving of God's help. We may feel angry with God, when, in the past, we pleaded and didn't get the results we expected. It's important to let go of pride and humble our selves. We can ask God to help direct us to the place in our body where we are storing up feelings that are keeping us blocked. Dialog with God. Write feelings down if it helps. Once you're done getting it all out, stop and listen. What is God telling you? Spend some time with what you hear or feel. Don't be surprised if the voice you hear is your own. Be assured the Holy Spirit is moving in it. At this point, you may already be experiencing lightness in your load. You may feel less alone.

*Discernment comes through prayer.* Pay attention to the voice of the Spirit within. This step calls for patience. Answers may not come immediately. Imagine a puzzle with all its pieces spread out on a table. The whole puzzle is laid out before you, and yet, it looks unrecognizable. You may see two pieces that clearly appear connected to one another and so you put them together. It's a start in the process of connecting the whole. We too must trust that God has the big picture and often gives us glimpses in the process of solving our spiritual and emotional dilemmas.

*Keep moving forward.* Despite not having all the answers we seek, once we have communicated with God through prayer, we trust our instincts to lead us in the right direction. We release anything that holds us up. We become aware of the next right move we need to make. This doesn't mean we forget or dismiss the unsolved problem. It does mean we don't allow it to control our being. Don't let worry rent space in your head. Trust your instincts to take you in the right direction. If it turns out you need to make another detour, you will be shown. Revisiting an issue may be necessary; however, reliving it to the point of exhaustion can be emotionally, physically, and spiritually damaging.

*Rest in God:* Believe that God is with you, in you, around you...everywhere present to you. When we have trouble believing in ourselves, God doesn't even flinch. Rest in that warm and generous Light.

**Ponder:** If you find yourself confused, bewildered, and back in your own head trying to solve your problem, go back to the drawing board. Erase your plans and put God back in the driver's seat. The solutions may take time;

however, we can trust God's presence in them. We may feel challenged, yet, filled with assurance, as the great mystic Julian of Norwich once said, "All shall be well." Is there something that needs your loving attention at this time? Use these steps and see what happens with whatever needs your present attention.

*Pray:* Dear God, I give you all my concerns and worries, problems and disappointments this day. Let me rest in you and always remain open to receiving your grace.

*Psalm 37:7*
*Luke 12:35-40*
*Lamentations 3:24-26*

# Gain Wait

*"Life isn't about waiting for the storms to pass...*
*it's learning to dance in the rain."*
Vivian Greene

**Pause and Reflect:** Has frustration and impatience caused you enough angst to curse out loud? Does your head hurt from the racing thoughts entering your already tired brain? Have you ever asked God,
"Why me, why now?"

We've all had questions and feelings that cause us to become confused and irritated. The problem is that often times we feel we must find solutions immediately and on our own. Waiting for answers is often difficult. We experience emotional distress in the not knowing.

The best solution is to gain wait!

First, it's helpful to express our feelings with God in the most honest way we can muster. Don't worry; God can listen to the most internally volatile words we express. No need to be polite; God takes us right where we're at. He knows what we are feeling anyway! Nothing is a secret from him. God would rather we have a real heart-to-heart conversation versus passivity, indifference, or dispassion.

Having emptied out our angst and concerns before God, we then ask God for help. Perhaps we are looking for a new door to open, to let go of old patterns, or to be inspired through prayer, meditation, and creative energy. God loves our petitions and never tires of our asking him for help.

Finally, we wait—patiently and attentively—with the willingness to accept what we cannot change and allow God to mold us according to his plan. Waiting on direction is not a passive activity. We go about our usual activity trusting that God's plan for us is unfolding in the people we meet, the circumstances we encounter, and the places we find ourselves drawn to. We make choices, we continue our conversations with God and we pay attention to the urgings of the spirit within us. We are actively participating in our recovery from emotional distress.

Here's a personal example of gaining wait. I hadn't been feeling particularly inspired during the Lenten season, a time for Christians when particular attention is paid to prayer, fasting, and almsgiving. A full schedule had me on the go with little time for attention to prayer and meditation. When I tried to paint, an activity that often is meditative, I found myself forcing it and getting nowhere. Even my prayer seemed superficial and I was easily distracted. Feeling like the season was passing me by, and I was failing miserably, I had no choice but to gain wait. I arrived very early for the Palm Sunday Mass and sat quietly talking with Jesus. I was aware of my drifting thoughts and gently made attempts to bring them back to some kind of spiritual focus with little success.

During the holiest of weeks, I found myself distracted, uninspired, creatively depleted and needing to go to the well to be filled. I had to make a choice about how I would respond to these feelings. I decided to open myself up to God's love and mercy. I asked God to help me remain patient and loving toward others and myself until the focus returned, the energy picked up, and the creativity began to flow again.

Meanwhile, there were things I chose to do. I read one line of scripture every morning and sat for five minutes in silence; whether or not an insight came to me was unimportant. I decided to get some fresh air every day. Every time a negative thought or old tape played in my head I acknowledged it and asked God to move it away and replace it with a positive thought. I recognized self-judgment as a useless ploy to distract me from the important things in my life. Somehow, just my noticing it helped me to feel lighter and more playful, and I was no longer taking myself so seriously. Slowly, my energy returned, my creativity increased and my prayer life felt more alive.

**Ponder:** Gaining wait has never failed so long as our hope is in God. We won't always understand his plans or his timetable and yet, trusting in him to walk with us through challenging times is an important part of our spiritual growth. We are a part of this plan; therefore, we can actively participate in our emotional healing.

**Pray:** Dear God, things may not always go the way I want them to go. Give me patience as I wait to feel you stirring inside of me. When I'm thirsty, fill me up with living water. Protect me from evil thoughts and shine your light so that I may follow your lead. Calm me as I wait for answers already inside me, which have not yet been discovered.

*Romans 8:24-30*
*Hosea 12:6*
*Psalm 25:5*

# Washing Feet

*"The True Church can never fail,
for it is based upon a rock."*
T.S. Eliot

***Pause and Reflect:*** I felt an incredible sense of anticipation and hope as I watched white smoke pour out of the Vatican chimney, signaling the election of a new pope. There were tears welling up from inside that I could not explain at the time.

As I look back, it began with Pope Benedict announcing his resignation. I felt such love and respect for this holy man. Through prayer and discernment he trusted the urgings of his heart and mind to God. One can only imagine the weight of this decision on his shoulders. I was so impressed with his humble spirit. This sincere gesture opened people's hearts to new possibilities in the Church.

That's what my tears were about, hope. We pray for leaders who are sincere, compassionate, just, and faithful. When Pope Francis bent down and asked the world to bless him, we saw his humanity and humility. I wonder if he, too, heard God whispering "Come Francis, rebuild my church" as did the saint whose name he chose.

Pope Francis asked for and received the blessings not only of Catholics but from people around the world. He understands that we're all in this together. He cannot rebuild a Church alone. Pope Francis, like Jesus, asks us to help wash each other's feet.

Rebuilding the church has nothing to do with buildings. It has everything to do with washing one another's feet. The symbolism of washing feet is to embrace, hold and give comfort. Our attitude must be one of humility and service. We can wash feet wherever we encounter people: in our homes, work places, schools, communities, and places of worship.

***Ponder:*** Here is a Top Ten List of ways in which we can wash another's feet:

Speak with kind words. Avoid swearing at people. It is demeaning. Stop using foul language on Facebook and in public. You may think it looks cool but actually it's immature and often offensive. Avoid any words used to categorize, label, or show intolerance toward a group or individual person. We build up a Church by not tearing people down.

Act with a kind heart. No matter how a person acts toward you, choose to act with patience, calmness, and a joyful spirit. Avoid taking things personally. Someone's poor disposition, bad day, or unbearable attitude is an opportunity for you to shine a light in a dark space.

Take time to pray for others. Remind yourself that God is present to everyone and in every situation. Rather than focusing on outcomes, pray that the will of God be accepted in all experiences.

Be present. Someone may need to share a vulnerable moment with you. Listen with your heart. Read between the lines. Ask a question that helps a person go deeper. Sometimes fewer words are necessary. We can hold a great deal in the silence.

Give joyfully of yourself. You are meant to share your time, talents, and treasures. What do you do well? You don't have to re-create yourself. The way you were created is enough. Share your gifts. The simplest gift is most often the most greatly appreciated. The receiver of the gift treasures the joyful intention.

Expand your capacity to love. Usually what we offer in sacrifice creates a joyful heart in us. Do something every day that demands no payment of any kind.

Intervene when you see injustice. Speak up. Act rightly. Pay attention to your gut instincts and the values you learned as a kid. It's easy to follow a crowd, yet, in the end, disquieting to live with an unsettled conscience.

Touch people. We have a tradition in which we extend a sign of peace to one another at Mass. It is a physical "reaching out" to offer hope and friendship to whoever is celebrating with us. I read recently that a grammar school has banned hugging by students. How sad! I say, offer your hand, a smile, a hug, an outreached arm around a shoulder. The world could use it!

Give alms; money or goods to help the poor. This is an essential part of service to those in need. We must become the hands and feet of God on earth. By serving those who are the poorest among us, we serve and honor God.

Invite people to the *table*. We share God's message of hope and love more effectively when we live our lives to the fullest and invite others to join us. Next time you attend a spiritual program, invite a friend or family member. If you know someone who is lonely, hurting, or feeling isolated ask him or her to join you for a family meal or outing. Encourage someone to take a walk with you. Offer to take an elderly person for an afternoon drive in the country. Ask someone to help you with a community service project. Many times people just need an invitation.

*Pray:* Dear Jesus, you have taught us with your words and deeds, "If I, therefore, the master and teacher, have washed your feet, you ought to wash one another's feet. I have given you a model to follow, so that as I have done for you, you should also do." (John 13:14-15). May we follow in your footsteps always.

*Romans 12:5-8*
*Luke 6:38*
*Mark 12:41-44*

# Make Mashed Potatoes

*" The church is the primary arena in which we learn*
*that glory does not consist in what we do for God*
*but in what God does for us."*
Eugene H. Peterson

**Pause and Reflect:** God's love and mercy are a gift, a grace. We can't earn it and we don't deserve it. It comes despite our shortcomings, faults, failures, and rebellious nature.

God will love us even when we forge ahead with our own plans, disregarding a process of discerning his will because we think we have all the answers. He loves us when we say, "I trust you completely," and then proceed to try and control everyone and everything in our day. When we think the grass is greener on the other side, and we wander off, rather than tending to our own yard, he still loves us.

We've heard it said so many times that there is nothing we can do that will cause God to turn away from us. Do you believe that with your whole heart and soul? Perhaps we've taken it for granted.

A woman shared this story with me: many years ago she noticed that her drinking began to interfere with her daily life. One day she decided to go to confession. She told the priest that she thought her drinking was out of control and that she might be an alcoholic. The priest apparently responded rather nonchalantly, "Why don't you go to AA and find out?" The woman was taken aback by what she considered the priest's casual response to her gut-wrenching admission. She told me, "It was like he was telling me to go make mashed potatoes!" While she thought the priest's response was dismissive, in fact, his suggestion was simple and direct. She ended up at an AA meeting and has been sober for many years.

More recently, the same woman was sharing about the losses she was experiencing around her husband's illness. He has dementia and is losing touch with reality. She spent an entire spiritual direction session blaming herself for what was clearly out of her control. She felt guilty that she was not doing enough. The hopelessness, anger, and sadness were apparent. Feeling utterly helpless myself, I listened, smiled, held her hand, and suggested, "Go make mashed potatoes!" She smiled, her shoulders slumped with a release of tension, and she breathed a sigh of relief remembering her own words.

**Ponder:** The point is that we can easily complicate already complicated lives. Sometimes we need to take a breath, relax, and let go. God hears our voices when we pray. His response to us is really quite simple and direct. Trust that you have what you need inside of you. I am present to carry you through a difficult time. There will be people around you that can help guide you.

Often, the answer is quite simple - not always easy - but simple. Next time you feel distressed, call upon God. Don't hesitate. And don't be surprised if you hear in a whisper, "Go make mashed potatoes!"

**Pray:** Dear God, sometimes life throws us curveballs we didn't see coming. In our moments of despair and frustration, anger and confusion, and any of our distresses, remind us of your presence. Give us the wisdom to hear your simple and direct words, "Trust me in all things."

*Psalm 18:6*
*Proverbs 16:3*
*1 John 5:14*

# Nature's Wisdom

*" God writes the gospel not in the Bible alone,*
*but on trees and flowers and clouds and stars."*
Martin Luther

***Pause and Reflect:*** I joined eight women whom I did not know on a daylong retreat at a seaside retreat center. I went to the retreat with the intention of leaving all my work behind. I purposely did not bring a computer, phone, book, journal or even a pen. I was going to let the Spirit move me. I got my wish!

It was a bit windy, cold, and damp, and a fine drizzle fell throughout the day. The sky and ocean water almost blended together in a steely gray color. Despite the chill in the air, I have always been drawn to this secluded beach for walks and thoughts. This day was no different.

After Morning Prayer and reflection the retreat leader played a musical meditation and then invited us to spend time with God, however we were moved to do so. My desire was to take a walk on the beach, but as the music played, all I kept thinking in my head was, "I don't want my hair to get messed up in the wind and rain!"

I remembered hearing someone once say that we have five seconds to make a decision about an internal desire before our brain begins to reason or talk ourselves out of it. Sometimes that's a necessary thing, but sometimes we ignore our desires just to "keep it safe." After four seconds I got up and walked outside, toward the beach.

After a long walk at the beach I began my journey back to the center. I noticed crocuses and daffodils, some budding and a few blooming. There was a pussy willow bush with branches so long and full they were drooping toward the ground. Patches of Spring grass grew in safely protected spots and trees were filled with buds still wrapped tightly into themselves.

I thought to myself, nature doesn't need to respond to the five-second rule. A tree is just a tree. It waits patiently for its time to bloom. The daffodils wait for the ground to thaw, the warming of the sun, greater length of light and for spring rains to quench their thirst. Perhaps they respond to the gentle hands of the gardener who delicately nurtures its soil.

We have the privilege of choice. We can choose whether to follow God's desire for us or not. We can engage in life's daily musings or not. The natural world invites us to play; we have the choice to engage or not. We have the freedom to be our true selves or not.

We certainly can take a few lessons from the trees and daffodils and the rhythms of the seasons. Perhaps we are called to be just who we are. God doesn't love us once we are who we think we should be, God loves us right where we are...warts and all. How wonderful it is when we can bloom in God's time and allow ourselves to be nurtured by others as well as by nature.

And how truly grateful I was to remember the five-second rule and to follow the Spirit's whimsical invitation to play and remain in the present moment.

*Ponder:* Today, take some time outdoors and linger a bit in nature's midst. Do not let cold, heat, snow, rain or sleet deter you. Let the elements, whatever they may be, delight your nature. Play, be quiet, dance, sing, walk, run...let yourself be free. Spend some time writing a few thoughts about how it felt being in God's playground? What did you notice while in nature that stirred your soul?

*Pray:* Dear God, may the beauty in nature that stirs my soul bring me into awareness of your constant presence and bounty.

*Genesis 1:11-12*
*Psalms 89:11*
*Acts: 17:4*

# Called to Serve

*" Prayer in action is love,
and love in action is service"*
Saint Mother Teresa

***Pause and Reflect:*** Mother Teresa said, "We are not called to be successful, we are called to be faithful."

Today, rather than worrying about whether we have enough stuff, the right stuff, the stuff someone else has, or if our stuff will make us richer, more beautiful or more famous, let's think about service to others.

Stuff isn't bad. This is not a reflection on the need to give up our stuff, rather, a suggestion to be mindful of our attachments to the stuff. Attachment to any thing, person, or idea tends to create a feeling of being stuck in cement boots. We find ourselves repeating the same worn out and unfulfilling patterns. We may find it challenging to move outside our comfort zone in giving service to those on the fringes of society.

Father Marc, a friend from days in Alaska, decided to go to Haiti to do what he could do for the very poorest children of that region. After arriving in 1998 he rented a house and took in several abandoned children. He became their mentor and teacher. Having given up all his material possessions he counted on the generosity of others to support his mission work. He trusted God, though I'm sure he faced unbelievable challenges and spent many sleepless nights worrying about where he would get the money to support these children, to get food and to provide shelter. He persevered through frustrations, sadness, and loneliness.

Father Marc was able to buy land in Les Cayes, located in southwestern Haiti. Today over 600 children eat a nutritious meal three times a day, attend school, learn job and agriculture skills, receive minimal medical attention and are spiritually nourished. Cinder block homes built by residents and volunteers provide the children with a solid roof over their heads.

Father Marc says when people come to Haiti they must realize that they are walking on holy ground. Why? I believe because you will be challenged. You will feel some discomfort. You will be among the poorest people in the world. You will be called to offer your gifts, hope, touch, love and compassion. Your educational degree won't matter; your social status will mean nothing and the amount of "stuff" you have will be of little consequence. The only thing that will matter is your heart to love, your hands to touch and comfort, your eyes to focus and your ears to listen.

These children are materially poor but spiritually they are rich. They smile, laugh, sing, pray and play. They love attention and love to give attention to one another. Despite their circumstances they are a grateful and faith-filled community.

There are many people experiencing spiritual poverty. They have lots of stuff but continually feel depleted and worn out. They often complain that they are too busy to pray and have little time for service. Distractions replace worship time.

***Ponder:*** We are not necessarily called to be Mother Teresa or Father Marc, but we are called by God to be faithful servants to one another. This week, if you find yourself too attached to your "stuff," take some time to check in with God. Perhaps you can ask for the willingness to serve others "in some small way with great love" as Mother would say.

Do you believe it is more important that you are successful or faithful? Why?

***Pray:*** Dear God, help us to recommit ourselves to your service here on earth, in every ordinary day, and in every ordinary opportunity given us.

*John 12:26*
*Hebrews 9: 13-14*
*Romans 12:10-11*

# Be Still

*"Whenever there is stillness,*
*there is the still small voice,*
*God's speaking from the whirlwind,*
*nature's old song and dance..."*
Annie Dillard

***Pause and Reflect:*** Several years back, on a particularly difficult day, I arrived at my spiritual direction session feeling a bit frazzled. My director sensed that I was feeling unsettled and helped me to process what was going on underneath the feelings. Then he asked me to close my eyes and suggested I listen carefully as he slowly repeated these words:

Be Still and Know that I Am God...
Be Still and Know that I Am...
Be Still and Know...
Be Still...
Be.

As he repeated each line slowly, my body, mind and spirit began to relax. I became mindful of God's presence within me. I was aware of a natural rhythm being restored. Since that time, I've used this mantra taken from Psalm 46:10 on many occasions.

It is our reminder that God can do things we feel unable to do alone. The spiritual calm that comes over us does not mean our problems have magically disappeared or that our concerns no longer matter. Rather, we have made a decision to place our trust in a Power greater than ourselves for daily direction on our journey.

***Ponder:*** Believing in God is not usually a challenge, but rather, trusting in God. Do you ever feel like you are on a merry-go-round that never stops? Today, if you begin to sense the imbalance, the dizziness of going around and around, the inability to stop the madness in your head, sit quietly and slowly repeat the words of the mantra to yourself. What practices help you to quiet your mind and open your body to conscious awareness of God's presence in your day? What is challenging about stillness? What is the reward of stillness?

*Pray:* Dear God, let my soul experience the invitation to be still and know you are present to me in this day.

*Exodus 14:14*
*Job 37: 14*
*Numbers 9:8*

# Blessed Be The Desert Experience

*"God takes everyone he loves through a desert.*
*It is his cure for our wandering hearts,*
*restlessly searching for a new Eden*
*...the best gift of the desert is God's presence*
*...the protective love of the Shepherd*
*gives me courage to face the interior journey."*
Paul E. Miller

**Pause and Reflect:** If your energy is low, if your days seem filled with uncertainty or fear, or if you feel lost and alone, hurt or uncared for, you may be having a desert experience.

Don't throw in the towel! You're in good company. Jesus, the saints, and our spiritual ancestors all had desert experiences. Perhaps it could be that we need to look at life a little differently during these times. Rather than close our eyes and fantasize about a better day, we need to open our eyes wide to a grace-filled experience. We are not alone in this experience even when it feels that way. God is engaging us, asking us to co-create a new vision. We need to participate in the experience with our whole body, mind, and spirit. Completely emptied, we focus our attention inward and listen for the quiet voice of God.

Sometimes our desert experiences feel uncomfortably routine; we become accustomed to them. We remain angry because to forgive may demand we let go of pride. We endure loneliness because to engage means we must risk. We endure fear because of its familiarity. Trust is challenging because it may mean abandoning old thinking. We cling to hurt and wear it as a false badge of courage, so that the world knows our suffering; we are fearful of what might happen should we let go of control.

God provides a way through the desert experience. In scripture it's called the *Holy Road*. This Highway of Holiness is God's plan to help us return from our exile and back to wholeness. The *Holy Road* is not always easy; however, it is the road of peace, contentment, trust, flexibility, openness, and love.

In taking this Holy Road we are asked to surrender ourselves to God's plan. We begin with prayer. Just begin to talk with God. Ask God to help you to conform your thoughts to his. Pay attention to your gut...what do you know to be right after placing God in charge? Accept that this plan may be a bit confusing to you. We are not supposed to have all the answers right now. Trust God has the big picture. Be assured he has carried the ball since the beginning of time. Ecclesiastes reminds us, "...whatever God does, that's the way it's going to be, always. No addition. No subtraction. God's done it and that's it." On this Holy Road we can cease fighting the *shoulds, becauses, if onlys, and maybe somedays*. God's got our back. We can relax.

You may experience a thirst and hunger you've never imagined. My friends, this is where the gift lies. It is in the emptiness that we can be filled. Old patterns and thoughts are of little use. We ask for mercy. We beg God to quench our thirst and hunger. The Holy Road is the place to purge ourselves of anything that keeps us away from God. And it is there that we are filled with all that we need to sustain us.

***Ponder:*** When we can say, "what I've been given this day is enough" we begin to experience wholeness. Grateful for a new attitude, we accept the desert experience as part of our journey. We trust that spring rains will come. Take a moment to reflect on a personal desert experience. What did you experience in the desert? What gift did you come away with from your experience? How has that gift changed you in any way? Now, spend a few minutes thanking God for all you have learned on the journey so far.

***Pray:*** Dear God, teach me to follow the Holy Road so that in all things I may find contentment and peace, especially during my desert experiences.

*Isaiah 35:1*
*Philippians 4:11-13*
*Isaiah 55:8-9*

# April

# Give Someone An OMG Moment

*"Be the reason someone smiles today."*
Anonymous

**Pause and Reflect:** While in Atlanta for our son's wedding there were so many very special moments, but one in particular stood out on the morning of the wedding.

My sisters and I decided to meet for breakfast at the Waffle House. (Please don't question my desire for a big, fat, heavy waffle on the day I needed to fit into my MOG dress!) For those of you unfamiliar with this restaurant, as was I until I reached Atlanta, the Waffle House accommodates about thirty people at a time. There is a counter that surrounds the grill and probably five booths for seating. The place is not designed for a large number of people to eat together. My brother-in-laws sat at the counter and we six girls squished into a booth designed for four people.

The place was mobbed. People were coming and going all morning. We had waited awhile to be seated in the booth. Once seated, the stories and laughter began. One of my sisters bought a new pair of glasses that became the butt of self-deprecation; it was all in good fun, and some of our most hilarious laughs.

It was clear to our waitress we were there for the duration. This was not going to be an "in and out the door" morning. This woman was working like her apron was on fire, serving people all over the restaurant. In the confusion, much of our order was messed up; little mistakes like wheat toast instead of rye, coffee instead of tea, sunny-side up rather than scrambled. We did insist on new waffles when she placed honey instead of syrup on the table and one bite told us something just wasn't right! Through it all, we continued to have a wonderful time and she was just as sweet as could be, making every-thing right. She bantered with us about the wedding and all kinds of things in between table-hopping.

Almost two hours later, finally ready to head back to our hotel, she came to the table announcing that our brother-in-laws paid our bill. We knew they had already left a good tip because, well, that's just what they would do. One of my sisters suggested that we try to make this server's day. We each dug into our wallets and pulled out substantial bills. We wrapped it together and handed it to her. She had no idea how much she had received. However, by the time we started to leave, she came back to the table and with tears in her eyes said, "You know you girls just gave me an OMG day!" It was hugs all around. The smile on her face and ours spoke volumes about the morning encounter.

We left having spent a wonderful time together as sisters. This wedding was the first in our family for our children. It was special in itself, but being with my sisters to share all that joy made it amazing. The ceremony and the reception were made all the more special with their support and love, but the Waffle House was what started off this very memorable day.

**Ponder:** My sisters and I so appreciate the gift of family, of laughter, and of sharing joy. To give someone an OMG day was just a little way of sharing our complete happiness with another person. When was the last time you had an opportunity to share your joy with others? To give back in a small way what has so generously been given to you by God? Make a conscious effort to surprise an unsuspecting someone by shining your light into their world. Perhaps you could pick flowers and deliver them to a friend's front door. Send a card to someone for no reason except to let them know you're thinking of them. Bring coffee to a coworker and while you're in line ordering, buy a coffee for the person behind you. There are so many simple ways to surprise someone today!

**Pray:** Dear God, in the ordinariness of this day, let me find ways to bring a smile into the heart of someone in need of joy and comfort. In me, may others see you.

*Psalm 126:2-3*
*1 Peter 1:8*
*Isaiah 55:12*

# We Are Called to Bear Beams of Light

*"People are like stained-glass windows.*
*They sparkle and shine when the sun is out,*
*but when the darkness sets in,*
*their true beauty is revealed*
*only if there is a light from within."*
Elisabeth Kubler-Ross

***Pause and Reflect:*** In his book The Awakened Heart, Gerald May asserts that William Blake was right when he said that the purpose of humanity is to learn to bear the beams of love. May goes on to say, "there are three meanings of bearing love: to endure it, to carry it and to bring it forth."

I can think of nothing more demonstrative of love than Jesus' passion, death, and resurrection. He loved deeply despite the cynicism, disrespect, betrayals, and denials. He did not ask anyone to change in order that he may love them; rather he accepted them with their shortcomings. Despite his emotional, psychological, and physical sorrow he accepted his cross without complaint. As he trudged the road to his death, he stopped along the way and accepted comfort and help. Before he died, he forgave those who tortured him. In total selflessness he gave himself over to God's will. In the resurrection he brought forth a new message of hope and love for the entire world.

May says, "we are meant to grow in our capacity to endure love's beauty and pain." Learning to breathe God in with all our senses helps us to appreciate more fully the gifts that grace us. Savoring our food, noticing the seasons in all their splendor, touching someone in need, and listening to that gentle voice inside of us are ways we honor God. The more mindful we are of life being "gift" the less chance we'll take it for granted.

We, too, must learn how to bear our crosses with dignity. When life is overwhelming and it feels like one blow after another, sometimes all we can do is surrender ourselves to God. In painful times it's OK to just be real, to be vulnerable, to accept help, and to let others expand their capacity to show love and compassion toward us. There are people in our lives who teach us more about living life precisely because they are willing to endure their pain and joy honestly and with gratitude for life no matter what it brings.

The Resurrection is not a footnote in history but rather a call to be bearers of love and hope to one another. It is a call to transformation and rebirth. It is a time for us to empty our tombs of resentment, anger, loneliness, fear and anxiety and find the light of God's grace within. We are then called to carry that light into every nook and cranny of our life.

*Ponder:* There is a wonderful sign at the end of our church driveway that reads: "Entering Mission Territory." You may want to write those words on several sticky notes and place them at work, on the refrigerator, in your car or wherever you need to be reminded that you are called to bear beams of light! How have you been a bearer of God's light today? How has the light of another person come to bear in your life in a way that has left a lasting impression on you?

*Pray:* Dear God, may your light fill me and spill out into every space I travel today.

*Matthew 5:14*
*John 12: 35-36*
*Luke 11:34-35*

# Living In The Now

*"Once I knew only darkness and stillness...*
*my life was without past or future...*
*but a little word from the fingers of another*
*fell into my hand that clutched at emptiness,*
*and my heart leaped to the rapture of living."*
Helen Keller

**Pause and Reflect:** If we want to understand our reactions and responses to present life circumstances, we can often look back and notice our patterns and experiences from childhood to the present. Our history explains a lot about us.

I was recently asked if it was important to know the why of things. If understanding the why helps us to accept others and ourselves it can be a powerful and transformational tool. However, the why cannot always be explained to our satisfaction. We must be cautious; if the why becomes so important that it holds us back from living in the moment it could be detrimental to our well-being. We cannot let the past be used as an excuse to hold onto guilt or shame or to hold us bound to old and useless patterns of behavior.

For example, recovering addicts understand the importance of living in the now. Early in recovery they may have spent a lot of time trying to figure out the whys and hows, but what matters is doing what is necessary to live a healthy life in the present. The whys of the past seem to be revealed slowly over time. There will always be mysteries that may or may not be revealed to us. We must not waste precious time focusing our energies on those things that are out of our control.

If we open ourselves to it, our faith in God plays a huge role in keeping us focused on the now of life. Place yourself in the trusting hands of God and all that needs to be revealed will be revealed. Be satisfied with what you know, trust your God-given instincts, hold out your arms to all of life's possibilities, gladly accept what you've learned from your past, and with gratitude surrender yourself to this moment.

Rather than asking why about our pasts, let's focus on the why nots of what is right in front of us.

**Ponder:** Make a Why Not list every day for a month: things you may think are far-fetched, or require a risk, perhaps a dream or desire. Make no demands; rather open yourself up to the possibilities. See what happens when you focus on the now of life. As you sit with the feelings arising in you now, how does your mind, body and spirit feel? Is there an unanswered question from your past that has resurfaced? How are you experiencing that question right now?

**Pray:** Dear God, help me to live in the present moment with deep trust in you that I'm exactly where I need to be.

*Ecclesiastes 5: 18-20*
*Isaiah 43: 18-19*
*Psalm 118:24*

# The Rhythm Of Life

*"Life has its rhythm and we have ours.*
*They're designed to coexist in harmony,*
*so that when we do what is ours to do*
*and otherwise let life be,*
*we garner acceptance and serenity."*
Victoria Moran

***Pause and Reflect:*** We've all experienced a moment while driving when a song plays on the radio that brings back memories from a past experience. Perhaps we remember the first song we danced to at our wedding, a lullaby we softly hummed to our children, the singing of "The Star-Spangled Banner" at a ballgame, a silly rendition of "Happy Birthday" sung at a party, or a favorite church hymn that stirred us.

The singing of birds at dawn, the sirens of bugs in the heat of the day, the whir of the wind, the croaking of frogs at dusk, the rustling of leaves, the rhythm of the ocean waves crashing onto shore and the groans of volcanic rock shifting remind us that nature, too, has her own melodies.

Our bodies silently play the tune of the Beloved. To feel its rhythm we need only gently press our fingers to our wrist, neck, or heart to feel the pulse that is the song of our life.

Music is an energy that can move us to tears, to dance. It sometimes irritates us, brings us joy or can make our hearts sing. We may not play a classical instrument or carry a perfect tune but we can appreciate the gifts of music, song, chant, or melody in our everyday lives.

***Ponder:*** Today, make time to listen to the music in your day. Show your appreciation for the wonderful gift bestowed upon creation. Thank God for the ability to feel and hear the rhythm of life. Say thanks to the talented people who create and play music for our enjoyment and stir us up a bit, the writer who touches our soul, the cook who delights our palate. Let's not take these rhythm creators for granted; rather let's celebrate them and their gifts!

Sing. Play. Hum. Whistle. Dance. Move. Feel. Listen. Remember. Appreciate. What rhythms do you notice in your daily life? How do these rhythms bring you closer to God?

*Pray:* Dear God, draw my attention toward your energy and rhythm so that my soul sings!

*Psalm 27:4*
*Matthew 11: 28-30*
*Ephesians 5:19*

# Time For A Change

*"The only way that we can live is if we grow.*
*The only way that we can grow is if we change.*
*The only way that we can change is if we learn.*
*The only way we can learn is if we are exposed.*
*And the only way we can become exposed is*
*if we throw ourselves into the open. Do it.*
*Throw yourself."*
C. Joybell C.

***Pause and Reflect:*** Have you ever heard these words spoken to you? "This is the way we've always done it." Do you sometimes have the same reaction I have?

"So bleeping what?"

Unless there is a very good reason to continue doing something over and over again the same way, my suggestion is to try something new and see how it works out. Try out a novel idea, something "out of the box," or put some pizazz into an old idea. Sometimes we just need to spice things up!

Repetition is good for us, no doubt. But when fear of change is our only reason for not considering switching things up, it's time to take a good look at things. Are we afraid someone's idea may get more credit than ours? Are we afraid of being wrong? Are we fearful that a new idea may require more effort?

I once read that our goals should be written in concrete and our plans in sand. Being flexible, open, and capable of adapting to new ideas shows a sign of vitality and spirit. Remaining rigid, especially with ideas that are not working for us, is a sure sign of death.

***Ponder:*** No more excuses! God wants us to live lives that are joyous, free, and whole. Repeat what needs to be repeated and show a willingness to give up the old and familiar if it's not working. If you surrender the process to

God you can trust his voice, move with the nudge, open yourself to the possibilities. Just because someone says, "that's the way it's always been done" doesn't mean it's necessarily the best or only way. You may be in awe of what God has in store for you! How do you feel when someone responds, "that's the way we've always done it," when you are considering a change? How are you responding internally to your own need for change?

***Pray:*** Dear God, help me to discern your will. Give me the courage and strength to make any changes necessary so that I may live into your plans for me.

*Joshua 1:9*
*Ecclesiastes 3:1*
*2 Corinthians 5:17*

# Talents and Gifts

*"Your talent is God's gift to you.*
*What you do with it is your gift back to God."*
Leo Buscaglia

***Pause and Reflect:*** She never took a single music or singing lesson. It's probably not so unusual for an eleven-year-old child. When it comes to opera, how many children her age would even know what that is, and, after listening to it, would say, "I want to do that!" However, Amira Willighagen accepted an invitation from musician Andre' Rieu to perform for an audience of seasoned patrons in the Netherlands.

Amira taught herself to sing using YouTube tutorials. Her voice is beyond amazing. She will be, God-willing, a superstar someday. She is already a sensation and her performances are riveting audiences. Her soulful voice is bringing people to tears and to their feet in thunderous applause. Find her on YouTube. It's suggested by YouTube editors that you turn away from the screen for a moment, and remind yourself you're listening to an eleven-year-old girl.

The point is, we all have gifts, purposes for which God has placed us on this earth. We all have raw talent of some kind given to us by our Creator. Amira must have experienced a calling. Something within her drew her to music. So, the question is, do you pay attention to what awakens and stirs in you?

After realizing her inner passion, this young, inquisitive girl responded to this calling by taking action. Amira didn't resist or deny the urge. She didn't make excuses for why singing would be impossible to pursue. How often have we acted upon our deepest urgings? Has fear or laziness stopped us? Have we told ourselves that it would be too difficult or too costly? Has perfection or comparisons to others put a damper on our time, creativity, talent, or initiatives?

Many of us will never experience the cheers of an audience in a theater. We may never receive accolades from around the world or have over a million hits on YouTube to recognize our accomplishments. My guess is that Amira's response to God's gift had nothing to do with stardom. I imagine her childlike heart responded to her calling simply because she was free to choose. Amira followed her heart and trusted her gut instincts. She was too young to burden herself with any self-imposed boundaries.

*Ponder:* There is a difference between gifts and wants. We can want a whole bunch of things, be denied, and come up feeling empty. God's gifts and desires for us come through grace for the service of others. The next time you feel an urging that brings you deep joy or a thought that seems to be filled with possibilities, explore it further. You may feel so moved by the urgings that you feel compelled to respond, or willing to receive this gift with a grateful heart. You may not fully understand what you are being called forth to do, but remain open to God working through you. What God sees as a gift may not seem to you purposeful; trust that it is. And, when others share their gifts, do not covet them in thoughts or misguided deeds. Rejoice with them. Don't let jealousy sabotage your spirit. God's varied graces are sufficient for us all. The size and depth and breadth of your gifts matter not at all to God. He knows your intentions well. Look only to serve the Gift-giver and you will be satisfied. What talents and gifts has God given you to share with others? Is there anything holding you back from pursuing or sharing a talent or gift with others? What changes can you make to let your gifts shine?

*Pray:* Dear God, thank you for the gifts and talents you have given to me. Let me always remember that they have been bestowed upon me so that I may share them with others in order to honor and praise you.

*Hebrews 13:16*
*1 John 3:17*
*Proverbs 18:16*

# May

# Multi-passions

*"But at the extreme, even strengths can become liabilities...*
*Since our projects are so much fun,*
*it's easy to push ourselves too far -*
*to sort of OD on them."*
Emily Wapnick

***Pause and Reflect:*** I met up with a friend at a wonderful little café for tea and conversation. We met several years back on an airplane while traveling south. At the time our paths crossed we were both in a similar place in our careers. We had left school jobs, she as an art teacher and I in campus ministry. At the time, neither of us knew exactly what the future held but we felt a calling to something *a little different.* In the past few years, although our visits are sporadic, we remain connected through social media and local events. We have become cheerleaders for one another when it comes to pursuing our dreams.

And so, on this morning, our conversation turned to future goals. We've come a long way in the pursuit of melding our work and spiritual lives together. We are blessed with a desire to continue learning through our successes and failures, and from the wisdom of mentors, teachers, and others sharing their stories and experiences with us. When it comes to our life's work, we seem to agree that we are trying to share our authentic selves with others. Whether in art, writing, public speaking, or anything we choose to do, the connection is made when a part of our story resonates with others. In that sharing, our passions are fueled and creativity is boundless. Our conversation lasted a couple of hours and I was grateful for the opportunity to remain connected and once again take away some nuggets of wisdom.

As I left the café my mind was filled with new and energizing ideas for the near future. "Hold on!" I said to myself, "this is a doubled-edged sword." I get excited and want to start executing a plan of action and then another, and yet another! It was the term multi-passions, which my friend brought up in our conversation, which continued to play in my head as I thought about new plans.

After all, aren't we encouraged to give attention to our passions? Are we not supposed to surround ourselves by those things we passionately love? Can we ever have too much passion? It was Dorothy Sayers who once said, "the only sin passion can commit is to be joyless." The warning may be that if we spread ourselves too thin, giving ourselves over to too many ideas and plans, as wonderful as they may be, we will divert attention away from the very thing we're called to nurture and grow.

I narrowed down the projects rolling around in my heart and head. In order to give these projects my best effort, and to see them through to the end with any chance for success, I had to look at my priorities. I needed to decide among my many passions which must be scaled back, even if temporarily.

As with any worthwhile pursuit, it requires focus. After all, the last thing we want is for our dreams and passions to become joyless and fraught with unnecessary anxiety.

**Ponder:** Sometimes taking a step back helps us to move forward. I'm reminded of a reading from scripture that says, "…the fruit of the Spirit is love, joy, peace, patience, kindness, generosity, faithfulness, gentleness… If we live in the Spirit, let us also follow the Spirit." Galatians 5:22. How have my passions been an insight into my life? Have my passions become a liability in any way? In order to experience balance in my life, do I need to step back from projects that are overwhelming me at this time?

**Pray:** Dear God, may I be able to discern daily, in mind and body, where the Spirit calls me forth to do the work necessary to fulfilling your calling for me. May my "yesses" delight you and when necessary my "noes" be an equally sacred response.

*Proverbs 14:1*
*Isaiah 28: 24-26*
*Corinthians 12:7-10*

# Super Charge Your Prayer Life

*"Our life is our prayer.*
*It's our gift to the universe,*
*and the memories we leave behind*
*when we someday exit this world*
*will be our legacy to our loved ones.*
*The best thing we can do for ourselves and*
*everyone around us is to find our joy and share it."*
Anita Moorjani

**Pause and Reflect:** One of the most frequently asked questions I get in spiritual direction is, "How can I pray more effectively?" My response often involves making prayer part of the fiber of our being. In other words, we must learn to live into our prayer. We do this by honoring, serving, loving, and praising God in all the things we do and say in our daily experiences and circumstances. Rather than making time for prayer, we pray into the time we are given. Here are three suggestions that may help us remain conscious of God's presence in our lives this day.

Come to God with a humble heart.

"Two men went up to the Temple to pray, one a Pharisee, the other a tax man. The Pharisee posed and prayed like this: "Oh, God, I thank you that I am not like other people-robbers, crooks, adulterers, or, heaven forbid, like the tax man. I fast twice a week and tithe on all my income." "Meanwhile the tax man, slumped in the shadows, his face in his hands, not daring to look up, said, "God, give mercy. Forgive me, a sinner." Luke 18:10-13

I feel somewhat defeated when I notice myself making poor choices or acting out old patterns of behavior I'd sworn off. Some days I feel stuck, unmotivated to pray. My pride and ego surface in times I least expect them. I'm learning to accept these red flags as gifts from God. Something in my body feels off kilter. It's not so important that I figure it out as it is to pray for God to help me align my will with his. I need to come to God with humility, not in humiliation. Humility is an understanding of my place in relation to God while humiliation smacks of judgment. Lots of wonderful things happen in my life when I'm walking, running, standing, sitting, and playing. The greatest position for receiving (whether figuratively or not) is kneeling.

Look with eyes of love.

"Long before he laid down earth's foundations, he had us in mind, had settled on us as the focus of his love, to be made whole and holy by his love." Ephesians 1:4

I think sometimes we are afraid to become holy. Yes, I'm convinced we believe becoming too holy makes us weird or different. We may feel unworthy of becoming holy. God focuses his love on us so that we will be made whole in his likeness. In the ordinary experiences of everyday life we have thousands of opportunities to see and feel God. In nature, in joy, in suffering, in boredom, in the sacraments, at home, work, and play. Stop and notice how God is speaking to you inside. Don't judge your reactions; rather pay attention to what God may be saying to you in the experience. Holiness comes when we align our will with God's and allow his plans to be carried out through us in the course of a day. God does not love us into a freak show…he loves us into our greatest potential.

Bring your bucket to the well.

"Everyone who drinks this water will get thirsty again and again. Anyone who drinks the water I give will never thirst-not ever. The water I will give will be an artesian spring within, gushing fountains of endless life. John 4:13-14

There was a time I begged God for relief from my personal anguish. I found relief. I asked God for many things over the years, a good husband, children, health for my family and friends, continued strength to muddle through life's daily challenges. I receive those gifts. What I notice today is that I ask for less and less. My desire is to know God's will for me. Being in the Presence of the Divine is amazingly joyful for me. Today, Jesus is a friend who sits beside me and chats with me. The visual and auditory may be what my mind conjures up; however, it is inside my body that I experience his loving presence. I feel the Holy Spirit in my guts. I'm learning to trust those urges that feel right for me. The God of Mystery urges me towards tolerance, peace, and love. For me, bringing my buckets to the well is as simple as saying, "God, let me know your will and give me the power to carry out your plan this day."

Is it always easy? No. I'm still tempted to go it alone, to try to fix what needs to be let go, or to control what is not mine to control. Sometimes, it's only when I find myself thirsting again and again, that I remember to go to the artesian spring within to be filled. Fr. Peter Campbell reminds us, "The issues are in the tissues." The answers are found within the body as well.

*Ponder:* Let's not complicate prayer today. Keep it simple. Remain humble, look at everything before you with eyes of love. Bring every question and concern and everything for which you are grateful to God. When you find yourself trying to control or manipulate someone or something, imagine yourself on your knees asking God for help. Surrender it all. God can handle every bucket we bring before him.

*Pray:* Dear God, make me an open vessel for your will in everything I do and say this day.

*Matthew 18:3*
*Romans 8:26-27*
*1 Peter 5:7*

# A Thousand Hearts

*"Inside, as with all things good in life,*
*beauty and love have the final word...*
*again and again the grace of God has shown me*
*that this is the way, what a joy-filled way."*
Excerpt from a letter written by my son Chris on his wedding day

**Pause and Reflect:** The marriages of both of our sons within four months of one another, to such beautiful women, inside and out, were truly a blessing to our family. Anyone who has experienced the gift of a loving partner for their child knows well the feelings of joy that come with this gift. This blessing doesn't just happen in a vacuum; it comes as the result of love being passed down through the generations. Hopefully, each of us has experienced this love from our parents, aunts, uncles, and cousins, who in turn learned it from relatives a generation earlier, and so forth. Ultimately, it is rooted in God's love for us. "And he is before all things, and in him all things hold together." Col.1:17

So, when my son's wife wrote in a letter that she hopes to honor our family in every day of their marrying, I believe her intent is to continue to pass along her love to family, friends, and all those God sends into her life. For those of us who continue marrying, we know there are lots of challenging times. It will take a thousand hearts to support these couples as they learn to co-exist, to raise a family, and to balance their work, play, and spiritual lives. They will learn to improve their capacity for patience, forgiveness, unconditional love, and perseverance. That happens when we come to know God is before all things and holds together all things.

A few years before my eldest son's wedding, I was at the receiving end of a phone call from a young woman totally devastated after my son broke off their relationship. It's not unusual for relationships to end, but this was particularly difficult because my son seemed equally devastated by his decision to end the relationship. He had been working as a strength coach in the NBA and feeling called by God in another direction. The question was, called for what purpose? Was it a call to the priesthood, to single life, married life, or to another profession or vocation?

I knew my son was struggling deeply with many questions and the turmoil of this break-up added a tremendous amount of stress to his situation. This tumult brought challenges he had never expected. As parents, we offered our support and love, but I must admit there were many days I felt helpless. There were evening phone calls that ended with great concern and questions on my part about my son's emotional health.

To hear this young woman's voice, her tears, her questions, and her deep hurt were so difficult. All I could offer was my hope that one day she would experience the joy God intended for her with the man of her dreams. I assured her of my prayers and thoughts. Months and months went by and our conversations ceased; however, my son was still struggling with many questions and choices about his life. Again and again, as I did with this young woman, I encouraged my son to trust God's plan for his life.

Turns out that both of these young people had further growing to do in order to discover who God was calling them to be. Here was a woman who thought she was in competition with God, an honest assessment from where she was standing. My son shared that, at times, he was feeling angry with God and unable to discern his direction. Totally understandable! It's amazing how God works in mysterious ways. Neither the young woman nor my son gave up on their faith. In fact, they found themselves depending on God and those God placed in their lives more than ever. After a year of discernment, God helped them re-find one another and strengthened their bond and commitment. In the end, my son made a decision to marry, and it was the young woman I tried to console on the phone who became his wife.

The days leading up to the weddings included individual hearts honoring these couples. Families mingled and blended and learned more about one another. But it didn't end there. In the days following the weddings we exchanged pictures, phone calls, and gestures of appreciation. We continue to extend invitations to reconnect. We pray for one another. We now have a common bond, a thread of love that is weaved from the fabric of each new life co-mingled with the married couples.

The events, the food and drink, the gowns and glamour, and the parties and music were all amazing. But above all these things, it is the love of family and friends that is enduring. God has blessed us with two very special bonds of love. While our newly married couples may honor us in their loving, we too honor them with our presence. We are called by God to support these couples as their journey of love continues through good times and bad, in sickness and in health, and everything in between.

Let me share a story that speaks to the heart of these family bonds of love. It was the day after my youngest son's wedding; the bride's family was hosting a barbeque at their Texas home. Unbeknownst to us, in the early morning hours, a tornado touched down in their neighborhood. Here they were preparing for family and friends to enjoy the day together before returning to their homes across the country, and they had no power. Their electricity would not come back on until the following day. This day could have had disaster written all over it, but, because of the love that was apparent in their family and friends, it turned out to be a wonderful time for all. No dire faces, no complaining, no cancellations, only an opportunity to get to know one another better. Friends and family laughed and shared stories into the wee hours of the evening.

With the sacramental vows completed and the wedding celebrations completed, we moved our separate ways and resumed our usual routines, but we have forever been gifted with change. This change is a new connection to family and friends who are connected to our children. The gift of family connectedness will continue well into our lifetimes and beyond.

*Ponder:* And so it is with God: beauty and love have the final word. Perhaps things don't always go as we plan, but God's Divine Timing unfolds as it is meant to be. Do you remember a time when your plans may not have gone as smoothly as you thought they might, yet rendered valuable gifts that have helped you become the person you are today?

What role has your family played in helping you to see God's love and beauty in all good things?

*Pray:* Dear God, may I honor you in all the special moments of family life. Help me to let love and beauty always have the final word.

*Ephesians 4:2*
*1 Peter 4:8*
*1 Corinthians 13:4-8*

# Dreams That You Dare To Dream

*"Hope is a waking dream."*
Aristotle

**Pause and Reflect:** Judy Garland sang a tune that has become iconic in American song lore. The words "dare to dream" from the song *"Somewhere Over the Rainbow"* may resonate with us. Children talk about their dreams. Parents encourage their children to follow their dreams. Adults teach children to work hard so their dreams come true. We tell children not to give up on their dreams. Dream big!

What happens when the dreams don't manifest as expected? Perhaps we work harder and longer to achieve the dream. We may believe others who tell us we aren't rich enough, talented enough, handsome enough, or intelligent enough for our dreams to come true. Feeling defeated after failed attempts at trying to make our dreams come true, we give up or stop believing in them.

Dreams can be based on magical thinking or soulful yearning. When we dream and leave the outcome in God's hands, the result is an abundance of opportunities. Detaching from the emotions and allowing our dreams to reveal something about ourselves may be fruitful. We cannot be disappointed in others or ourselves when we leave the results up to God. A dream may be delayed or not granted because God has other plans.

Dreams may seem to be wishful thinking, fantasy, or even unrealistic, but they also give us hope. It's not the dream that causes disappointment; it is our expectations of the outcome. So long as we continue to live in the present moment, we can allow our dreams to float about in the universe and ride the waves of energy surging around us. Daring to dream can bring about new awareness and opportunities beyond our wildest imagination.

Let your dreams inspire you. Allow God to give them direction in whatever form he sees fit. Hope is an awesome feeling. We cannot change the reality of the present, but we can dare to dream about possibilities. And when the Spirit moves us, we can respond with a resounding "Yes!" toward whatever it is we feel moved to do. Be careful not to etch your dreams in stone, but rather to let them float on the clouds close to God.

***Ponder:*** Our dreams are ever shifting and changing. Go ahead and dare to dream, dream big, and let God surprise you with his dream for you! What dreams do you dare to dream for your future? What do your dreams reveal about your desires?

***Pray:*** Dear God, you know my deepest dreams and desires. May they be in alignment with your will for me today, and give me hope for tomorrow.

*Matthew 7:8*
*Proverbs 3:5-8*
*Psalm 20:4*

# Joyful Sacred Space

*" As you proceed through life,
following your own path, birds will shit on you.
Don't bother to brush it off.
Getting a comedic view of your situation
gives you spiritual distance.
Having a sense of humor saves you."*
Joseph Campbell

***Pause and Reflect:*** Are you taking life a little too seriously? There is something unmistakably beautiful about a heart that is happy, joyous, and free!

We can hear our Gentle God asking us to bring our worries and discomforts to him. God wants to give us peace and contentment. He wants us to feel unchained from burdens that weigh us down. God more than anything desires that our bodies, minds and spirits feel free to soar with joy. Not necessarily a *happy, happy* joy, but rather the joy that resides deep within in us, *contented* joy.

Just for today, open yourself up to the delightful surprises God has in store for you.

If changes are taking place in your life, rather than fearing them, welcome the transition. Imagine all the opportunities for growth that will be coming your way.

Perhaps you have dreams that are buried deep within. Allow yourself to hope once again that your dream may become a reality. Even go so far as to open new doors of possibilities for your life. Go ahead...just imagine!

Are there companions you've yet to meet along your journey? Sometimes our shyness keeps us from approaching others we are interested in. If you want to know more about someone, just ask. And, give others an opportunity to know you better.

Joy must be given away. Compliment others. Express your gratitude. Share a lighthearted moment with a stranger and see how good it makes you feel inside.

Often, I choose to close my programs with music. People join hands and the prayerful, joyous melodies begin. Inevitably, they sway to the music, and eventually can't help but dance. It's wonderful to see people pray joyfully and freely.

*Ponder:* A dear mentor once shared this with me: there is only a one-letter difference between play and pray. Sometimes we pray with such intensity we forget to relax and let go. It is when we let our hearts sing and dance and play and laugh that we open up and God pours himself into those sacred spaces. Can you think of anything better than a joyful, sacred space?

Feeling too serious? Take a deep breath. Let go of everything that seems to have a chokehold on you. Give it all to the Gentle God who has a few surprises in store for you today!

*Pray:* Dear God, give me the opportunity to laugh at myself today. Help me to better understand the difference between life's serious moments and taking life too seriously.

*Micah 6:8*
*Psalm 139:14*
*Ecclesiastes 5:18-20*

# Spiritual Makeover

*"Being at our least grateful, our pissiest and most self-obsessed, may create enough pain that we remember to do the footwork, get out of the house, or reach for the phone, or to get on our knees, or to get the hell outside."*

Anne Lamont

**Pause and Reflect:** You've been there. Those moments when you are so fed up with you, you need a break from yourself or else! The make-up does nothing for you; it's going to be a bad hair day despite all your efforts. Nothing the boss says will appease you. Despite your spouse's efforts you wish you were on an island alone for just one day, and the things you once touched that seemed to turn to gold now seem to tarnish. The list could go on and on but I think you've got the picture.

It's time for a spiritual makeover! Rather than asking God to change things, maybe it's time for acceptance and gratitude for all the gifts present in your life?

Perhaps one of the following ideas can help shift your perspective today:
- Thank you God: I am alive!
- Maybe my ideas don't hold the only solution.
- Act as if I'm surrendering the idea that "it's impossible."
- "Why not?" I'm going to take a risk.
- Putting aside my pride, I can look at my shortcomings.
- I will share real feelings rather than superficial thoughts or words.
- I will expect amazing and beautiful and awesome things today.
- I will seek self-worth from within not from others.
- Whether others deserve it or not, I will speak kindly and with compassion.
- I will simply notice the old tapes that play in my head. More than likely, they are not my present truth.

- Discomfort puts me in touch with what I need.
- Possessions do not further the work inside.
- I need to change no one today.
- I will intentionally seek places of peace both within and outside myself.
- I desire to live sensibly rather than satiated.
- I do not seek to master disciplines; rather, I allow them to unfold with gratitude.
- I will revel in simplicity.
- I promise to practice what I preach.
- I will laugh at myself and with others, rather than judge.
- Defiance is a roadblock, so I'll find a detour.
- My illusions can be replaced with enlightened thoughts.
- I will search for the confluence of religion and spirituality rather than berate either.
- I will remember Mom's words, "This too shall pass."
- I will listen to the stories my body wishes to share with me.
- I will value the wisdom of my seasoned friends as a treasure richer than gold.
- Forgiving another transforms me.
- Guilt is a teacher; shame takes me prisoner. I desire to live free.

**Ponder:** If today you are feeling a little miffed, self-absorbed or ungrateful, make a decision to accept those feelings, turn yourself over to God, and move forward. Perhaps a mini-mantra from the above list resonated with you. Maybe you found your own words. For today, live them from this moment on. Settle on a "no excuses" day. A spiritual makeover begins like any other makeover by looking directly into the mirror. What mantra have you chosen for this day? Why?

**Pray:** Dear God, help me to believe that I am beautifully and wonderfully made by your hands. Let my inner light shine today.

*Song of Solomon 4:7*
*1 Peter 3:3-4*
*Psalm 139:13*

# God Breaks Into Our Lives

*"The soul can split the sky in two
and let the face of God shine through."*
Edna St. Vincent Millay

***Pause and Reflect:*** On a warm August evening, my husband and I had been out to dinner, and stopped at a local hardware store for a gardening tool. After purchasing our item, we left the store, and were headed to our car. Standing in the parking lot we noticed an elderly man standing next to a hand dolly stacked with several bags of small stone, sand, and rebar. The man, of Asian decent, and unable to speak English, motioned to my husband that he needed help. I continued on to our truck, and my husband walked over to help the man unload his supplies into his vehicle. As I turned around I noticed both men walking toward our truck, my husband with a quizzical look on his face. It turns out, the older man had no vehicle, and was asking through hand gestures if he could load the materials onto our truck and get a ride to his destination. While a little skeptical, my husband and I nodded to the man that we would take him and his supplies to his destination.

The older man sat up front in the truck, and with the point of his finger began gesturing directions to my husband. It was about a two-mile drive to the elderly man's neighborhood. It was a simple house, meticulously kept. As the two men unloaded the supplies, I noticed that the driveway was being completely renovated in sections. After the supplies were unloaded, the man graciously offered my husband all that he could, water from his hose to wash his hands.

It was clear that this gentleman had made several trips to the hardware store to purchase enough supplies to complete one section of his driveway at a time. As we drove away, I wondered how many times he walked the two miles up and down hills with his hand dolly in the heat of the early evening. Did he walk home with his heavy load if unable to hitch a ride? How lovely it was to see the care this man took with his home, and the gentle spirit of his simple offering of water.

***Ponder:*** It's easy to be cynical about people, to put labels on those we don't know, to judge groups of individuals, and then God breaks into our lives and lets the sun shine through. God gives us a glimpse of what it's like to be our best human selves despite our human condition.

The baby, the Christ-child, breaks into our human condition and gives us glimpses of our God. This Son of God, love's pure light, fills us with surprises. May we all be led by the Light of the World, toward our best selves.

***Pray:*** Dear God, may the light of your love burn in our hearts so that all of humanity may see you through us.

*1 John 4:19*
*John 15:13*
*1 Corinthians 13:13*

# June

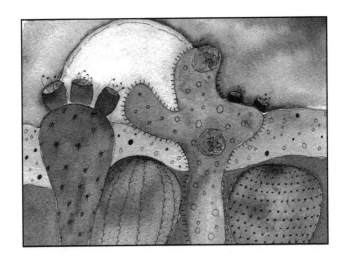

# Summer Solstice

*"I question not if thrushes sing, if roses load the air;*
*beyond my heart I need not reach,*
*when all is summer there.*

John Vance Cheney

**Pause and Reflect:** I jokingly sent a text message to a friend in Alaska as I watched the sun set on a most gorgeous solstice night in New England. The text began, "Why is it I think of you every summer solstice?"

Of course, I knew the answer to that question. We shared so many fun experiences as a tight-knit group of women on the island. Summers in Alaska were filled with a unique and special light, God's natural beauty shining for hours upon hours, and the other kind of light that came in friendships. We tended to linger longer on front porches (with a pitcher of margaritas), beside a river with a fishing pole at midnight, lying on the floor of our friend's yarn shop at five o'clock in the morning after a gals' night out in town (we needed the rest before returning home to the kids, and husbands!), and hikes up mountain trails. There were countless other delightful summer recollections, some of which are better left in the river of memories rather than written!

In response to my text, my friend called me as the sun shone brightly on the island. More than likely she forgot about the time difference, and I was already fast asleep. Frantically, I fumbled toward the sound of the rings, as they seemed to echo throughout the quiet hall. I happened to be working at a silent retreat. I whispered hello and finally found a quiet room downstairs to chat and catch up. An hour and a half later, after having shared family stories, we said our good-byes.

These are memories of the heart that will forever bring a smile and feelings of joy to my entire being. People who know me say I light up at the mention of time spent in Alaska. We are a group of women from all walks of life that in essence became lifelong soul sisters in a short period of years.

I've always said our life on the island was like a throwback to the 50s. No one had keys to their front doors. They were left open in case a neighbor needed to borrow something! High school proms were still held in a beautifully decorated gym. Our children played outdoors from sun up until sundown (which in the summer seemed endless). We never seemed to worry where they were because they traveled in groups awaiting the adventures of the day. Everybody looked out for each other. We gathered for evening cookouts in the "fishbowl," an area smack in the middle of our neighborhood. Many a therapy session took place on long walks and talks around the peninsula. I often thought world leaders would probably benefit from our style of problem solving!

They say once you've lived on an island you'll never be the same. Perhaps there is something very truthful in that. It changes you. It helps you to understand just how connected we really are to one another. There is an appreciation for times of gathering and companioning. As well, we understood the need for private moments in a place where truly everybody knows your name. One develops a healthy respect for nature in its most pure form, the beauty, the rawness, the delight, and the danger. Gratitude for the very simple pleasures abounded. It was a thrill to see an eagle spread its wings as it rested on a sandy beach, have a sea lion swim alongside the shore as you jogged in the early morning, watch a momma bear and cubs from a safe distance, or simply walk the beach and discover thousands of pieces of sea glass.

While on my retreat weekend I heard a priest reference the poet Henry James during a sermon. He said James once stated that the two most beautiful words in the English language are *summer afternoon*. Until that moment, I never thought about those two words in spiritual terms, but when he said them, my body resonated with sheer joy.

Ahhh... Summer solstice. Summer afternoons. Friendships. Memories. They are all significantly sacred within my body. Perhaps all are one in the same, of light and love, of God.

*Ponder:* Perhaps today is not a solstice. In mind and heart, recall places whose memories bring you joy and peace. Places that remind you of those two beautiful words, summer afternoon. Recall reminiscing with someone about a special time you shared together. What sentiments came forward for you? How does it make you feel, in your body, to remember this conversation or these sentiments?

*Pray:* Dear God, let a summer afternoon memory delight my heart. May your light bathe me in warmth and love regardless of today's circumstances.

*Exodus 20:8*
*Philippians 1:3*
*Ecclesiastes 9:7*

# Channeling My Inner Introvert

*"For me, chief among the joys of leaving the corporate world
and entering Jesuit novitiate in Boston
was the slowing down of my life.
I had spent six years working days, nights, and weekends,
so my introduction to the daily schedule, or ordo,
of the novitiate was a welcome change."*

James Martin, SJ

***Pause and Reflect:*** I can appreciate the results of the personality and assessment tests I've taken throughout the years. For me personally, they have not been surprising. I'm an adapter, feeler and perceiver with a desire for connectedness, positivity, harmony and empathy. I'm also an over-achiever who tends to drive myself to exhaustion, I'm an approval addict, and I like good results and have little patience for inefficiency. Since childhood I've been described as an extrovert. I am energized by interactions with people, I'm usually speaking as I'm thinking through things, and social situations are engaging for me. People have described me as gregarious, outgoing and friendly and yet, failure is difficult to accept, I doubt myself, and I can be very competitive.

While I better understand the extrovert in me, I'm discovering my inner introvert. She desires quiet spaces, no crowds, small gatherings, and enjoys one-on-one conversations.

As I mature and my spiritual life deepens, I'm finding myself being pulled toward solitude and thoroughly enjoying it. Being energized by hours of painting, spending time reflecting on scripture or a good book, walking alone in the woods or by the seashore, driving long distances by myself or attending an activity solo are very routine occurrences for me at this time in my life. As a matter of fact, I often prefer it to a flurry of people and activity.

Leaving the workplace five years ago was somewhat scary in that I no longer had a title, a steady paycheck or a daily routine. I no longer had the interaction and attention of colleagues on a daily basis. Yes, there are times I miss that, but overall I'm finding myself settling into a slower pace. Someone recently commented that I seem busier than ever! I rarely use the word busy to describe my life. Busy, for me, conjures up thoughts of mindless activity that is done at a hectic pace. Today, I tell people my days are full. Don't get me wrong, I still experience busy-ness, but overall my days are filled with moments of peace, quiet, reflection, service and mindful interactions.

***Ponder:*** We make choices in our lives that ultimately affect the quality of our lives. Listen to your body, pay attention to your senses, mindfully engage techniques that bring your mind to a quiet place.

Begin to see the fullness of life rather than its busy-ness. The introvert within just may need a voice.

Initiate just one change in your schedule that may help you to linger in the gifts God intends for you. How does it feel for you to anticipate making this change?

***Pray:*** Dear God, changes are so important in deepening my spiritual life. Help me to welcome changes and trust that you are always present, even in my unknowing.

*2 Timothy 3:16-17*
*Philippians 2:2*
*Lamentations 3:27-28*

# God's Doorway

*"When we open the door to the true self,*
*we uncover more of the sum of who we are.*
*Initially, this may lead to discomfort instead of peace,*
*for not everything we find is what we want.*
*But if we befriend what is within us and*
*are willing to learn from it, serenity*
*will ultimately reign at the center of our being."*
Joyce Rupp

***Pause and Reflect:*** I began to journal over thirty years ago. It was therapeutic to write my feelings down in response to the circumstances of my day. Initially, my journal contained what appeared to be a log of daily activities. Eventually, as I learned to go deeper, the circumstances became less important than the responses to them. I thought the goal was self- improvement. What I've come to learn is that my life is all about letting God improve me.

How does God want me to respond, or not? Where is God taking me in a particular situation? How are my shortcomings and undesirable traits teaching me a valuable lesson? Am I listening to the movement of the Holy Spirit within me? Is my response honoring, serving, praising and loving God?

Self- improvement is not my job. If my focus in everything I do, say, feel, and sense is centered on God's will for me then improvement of the self is the outcome. Personal improvement happens as a gift from God. It can happen regardless of status improvement, social improvement, environmental improvement, or anything else the outside world may measure us by.

Our only response to this day should be to open the door of our heart. Empty our head of all the needless distractions and concerns that begin to occupy space. Find time for quiet. Allow ourselves to receive whatever it is the day offers to us. And as we receive it, accept its Mysterious Unfolding. God is present to us no matter what the outside world throws at us.

While this may sound warm and fuzzy, I assure you it's not for the faint of heart. You will come up against some harsh realities. God may take you to places you'd rather not go. And make no mistake about it; these are not necessarily foreign places to you. God may ask you to open a door to a family member, a co-worker, a boss, a friend, or stranger. The door may swing open to anger, resentment, loss, illness, confusion, or pain. As you enter the door you may feel yourself overcome with familiar or perhaps new feelings. Your reactions may or may not be well thought out. The opposite may also happen. That door may swing open to joy and compassion, love and serenity, or curiosity and creativity.

When the unexpected happens, when the unwelcome happens, do we just shut the door on the experience or do we open ourselves up to trusting God to see us through? Lots of times rather than feeling the difficult or unwanted feelings we shut the door on them. Trouble is, whatever *it* is remains locked behind the door waiting for a vulnerable moment when it can cause havoc.

And when the doors of joy and creativity swing open, are we willing to receive them, bless them, and pour them back out into the world? Some squander gifted opportunities because they feel they don't deserve them, or they don't even recognize them. Sometimes we're so busy we don't notice the open doors.

I've found by opening the door and welcoming whatever it is, negative power decreases and positive energy increases. By trusting God to be with me in it, I maintain an inner peace and balance. I don't have to become too elated, nor do I have to fear. I pray to recognize God's presence and to help me face whatever is beyond the door.

***Ponder:*** We come to understand that our Beloved provides many doors. We must stand ready and willing to open them. And sometimes, when we seem overcome and unable to muster the strength and courage to open the door, God enters our private hell. We are shown a new way, in spite of our fear or hesitance, to nurture ourselves into wholeness. This, my friends, is grace. What do I need from God, others or myself in order to open the door to every opportunity intended for me to receive this day?

***Pray:*** Dear God, open the door of my heart so that I may embrace whatever is behind the door you've opened for me today.

*1 Corinthians 16:9*
*Revelations 3:8*
*Matthew 7:7*

# The Right Order Of Things

*"He must become greater and greater,*
*and I must become less and less."*
John 4:30

**Pause and Reflect:** In the Catholic faith, the celebration of the Solemnity of the Birth of John the Baptist began around the year 506. It was celebrated much like Christmas with three masses; a vigil mass, one at dawn, and again at midday. It comes three months after the celebration of the Annunciation, and six months before the birth of Jesus. We recall in the story of the Annunciation, John, upon hearing Mary's voice, leapt in his mother Elizabeth's womb for joy.

Always keeping Christ as the center, some say there is significance to the celebration falling around the solstice. Recalling the words of John the Baptist with regard to Jesus, "He must increase. I must decrease."

The stories read at the vigil mass remind us of the difference between the Creator and the created. They remind us of what it means to humble ourselves before God. It is about decreasing our egos, our wants, our fears, and our attachments to things that don't really matter. We pray for an increase in trust, faithfulness, patience, and perseverance.

Jeremiah tells us of God's intimate understanding and love for us, "I knew you before I formed you in your mother's womb." Our spiritual journey is meant to reconnect us with the God who formed us, touched us, molded and created us even before we came into this world. God never disconnects from us, but we often become distracted. Deep within each person, whether it is recognized or not, we crave an intimate reconnection with our Creator. Whether in prayer, quiet, joy, suffering, sacrifice, blessings, or service, we crave closeness to God. We desire God to increase in our lives. Or do we? Our sole responsibility is to become "respondable" to God. To seek out his will for us and to follow it.

This isn't always easy. Often, we are tempted to increase ourselves. Call it pride, stubbornness, old patterns, confusion, or the inability to understand what needs letting go or taking up, we feel the responsibility to fix everything ourselves. We become exhausted with effort. We may be paying more attention to the voices in our heads trying to convince us that we're not good enough, strong enough, not pretty enough or talented enough to live out God's magnificent dreams for each of us.

The fear of failure and self-doubt grows. We may become convinced that to risk change will bring about complete failure, embarrassment, and rejection. We are enticed by more, bigger, and better alternatives. This does not satisfy the soul, and so we continue to crave reconnection.

God knows we will be tempted and distracted. He knows life will be painful and confusing at times. Many of us have experienced the loss of a loved one, extended periods of illness, months and perhaps years of sacrificing to care for an aging parent. We have known the ache of addiction in our families or ourselves and have endured separation from a family member or friend due to misunderstanding.

There will be moments we fail to see God in the discomfort or turmoil. But the God that knows every detail of our being is there to help and guide us if we are willing to let go, to decrease and to let him increase in us. We must let go of pride and turn ourselves over to a plan that we may not always understand. It is in that surrender that we will come to know that our difficult times are opportunities for joy. Not the "Oh, I'm so happy" kind of joy, but the joy that comes deep within when we trust God no matter what!

Scripture tells us that the parents of John the Baptist surely understood pain and difficult times. They had their shortcomings, but they were devoted to God. After years of being unable to conceive a child, and during a time when couples were thought to be cursed by God if they were childless, they remained faithful. Can you imagine the alienation they must have endured? Ultimately, they trusted God's plan. They teach us about faithfulness and perseverance in the face of difficulty.

And God bore them a great gift in their son John. This gift then goes out into the world and embodies God's great mercy and love. He calls us to be mindful, to listen, and to answer God's personal call.

***Ponder:*** Deep inside each of us is a place of safety and familiarity, a place where God can reach us. It is a place where we can leap for joy as we reconnect with the Beloved One who knew us before we were formed in our mother's womb. Let us decrease those things about us that are not of God and allow God to increase in us. Today, let us celebrate becoming smaller as God becomes bigger in our lives. It is only then that we will be able to hear who it is God is calling us to be. Who is God calling you to be? What needs to increase in your life? What needs to decrease?

***Pray:*** Dear God, teach me to become a humble servant willing only to do what you desire of me today.

*2 Chronicles 7:14*
*1 Peter 5:5*
*Micah 6:8*

# Financial Serenity

*"Not having money to spend doesn't mean
we can't have well-spent moments everyday."*
Sarah Ban Breathnach

**Pause and Reflect:** Many of us fiercely pursue financial security, when in fact what we really hunger for is financial serenity.

What's the difference, you might ask? I'm certainly not a financial genius, so this isn't about the *numbers*. It's about attitude. Financial serenity is an inside job.

While I was growing up, I'm pretty sure my parents lived from paycheck to paycheck. My mom was a whiz at stretching a dollar and seeing to it that we had what we needed (not everything we wanted). I honestly never remember worrying about money or feeling like I lacked for anything as a child. My parents' focus was on the abundance we shared within the family, our faith, and our community. At my dad's retirement celebration, I remember being struck with emotion as his colleagues, one after another, shared stories about his generosity. He was a high school principal; my mom did not work outside the home and they were raising seven children...not the ideal scenario for amassing a fortune! Not only did my dad take the time to visit families at their homes after school hours, helping them work out issues and concerns, but teachers talked about him buying bicycles for children whose families could not afford them. My parents were content with what they could provide. They didn't let money worries consume them.

Looking back, I see how attached I became to my first paychecks. I wasn't particularly generous with my money. Although I hate to admit this, to some extent I did see money as a means to buying happiness, freedom, and self worth.

As my spiritual life was strengthened, I began to see money as energy that is meant to be earned and shared, always fluid, always moving. I found myself learning to detach from the negative power and influence of money. The

112

distribution of money will never be fair. Rock stars will always be paid more than teachers. When both are living to their full God-given potential, the arbitrary numbers in their paychecks do not define them.

We must try not to make money so important that we feel dependent upon it for our happiness. No matter what thing we have in our lives as a result of what money can buy, if we're not sharing it with others, it means so little. We must be aware of attaching worth—our own or that of anyone else's — to money. Money can never be the measuring stick of human potential and value.

Living the good life is an extension of inner peace and contentment. All the money in the world cannot buy that. Cynics might balk, but those with experience and wisdom know the truth.

Financial serenity means detaching oneself from the false sense of power one may experience with money. No amount of wealth can buy serenity. Our self-respect, capacity to love, generous spirit, and self worth are dependent on God's grace alone.

***Ponder:*** Pay attention to your relationship with money this week. Notice how you use it, spend it, give it, and receive it. Take a sincere mental and moral inventory around your present attitude toward money. Commit to making the necessary changes in your attitude; pray for a generous spirit and thank God for the blessings that are yours. Explore your feelings regarding financial serenity. On a scale of 1-10, with 10 representing the most serenity, where would you say you are? Is there anything about financial serenity that needs your attention?

***Pray:*** Dear God, May I find the worth of others and myself in seeing everyone as you see them, capable, talented, and deserving of love.

*Hebrews 13:5*
*Matthew 6:24*
*Proverbs 13:11*

# Spiritual Discipline

*"Spend your time and energy in
training yourself for spiritual fitness.
Physical exercise has some value,
but spiritual exercise is much more important."*
I Timothy 4:7-8

***Pause and Reflect:*** It requires a certain amount of discipline to keep our bodies fit. Rest, exercise, eating a balanced diet, drinking plenty of water, strengthening the core, and stretching all the muscles of the body are part of that discipline. While we may be well acquainted with what it takes to get into good physical condition, we may not always choose to do what is required to maintain it.

Discipline is that dirty little word that sometimes conjures up thoughts of pain, relentless work, punishment, and self-control. The words easy and discipline are rarely used in the same sentence when talking about exercise. It's true; it takes focus and effort to develop or improve our physical bodies, and the older we get, the more challenging it becomes!

How much time do we spend in a day caring for our spiritual fitness? God cares about our whole being. God created our bodies, our vessels, for carrying out all life's activities. However, God does not manipulate our bodies like a marionette on the strings of a puppet master. We are free to make choices about caring for our mind, body, and spirit-the whole vessel.

The wonderful paradox about spiritual fitness is that while it does require our attention, we don't have to go through mental and physical gymnastics to become more fit. It's not about taking more control; it's about letting go. It's less about self-improvement than it is about God-improvement. The repetitions are gentle; no one is judging and mistakes are opportunities for growth. Let God become your strength coach!

The goal of spiritual fitness is the intentional movement toward trust in God. Discipline taken to the extreme becomes punishment. God is constantly pursuing a relationship with us. We are invited into this relationship through love and mercy. God can deepen our desire and depth of trust in him. God wants to reach every fiber of our being with joy and truth.

The fact that, at times, we experience pain, loss, confusion, darkness, and loneliness is a good reason to strengthen our spiritual lives. We're more apt to call on God when things aren't going quite so well in our lives. Spiritual discipline, especially when we are feeling strong, prepares us for times of weakness and reminds us that when life is stressful we can turn to our Strength Coach to give us what we need.

We absolutely need to nurture and care for our physical bodies. Eventually, despite all our efforts, our physical bodies will die. The spiritual body has an eternal journey, so it's probably a good idea to spend a little more time each day paying attention to our spiritual fitness.

*Ponder:* Daily prayer, conversation, and listening to God help us to remain aware of a constant loving presence in our lives. Meditation helps us to clear our heads of useless chatter. By emptying ourselves of ourselves, we open ourselves to God's will for us. The distractions, drama, opinions, worries, and plans taking up space in our heads can be quieted in order to receive whatever wonderful things God has in store for us. Practices such as focusing, yoga, guided meditation, contemplative prayer, centering prayer, lectio divina, and walking a labyrinth are used by people around the world to practice daily spiritual fitness. Is there a spiritual discipline or routine that helps move you intentionally toward God? Share an idea or thought about your spiritual fitness routines. What works for you?

*Pray:* Dear God, open my mind, body and spirit to new ways of encountering you in my daily rounds. Let these new spiritual practices become part of my routine, so that in times of trouble or doubt, I can turn to them to find you.

*1 Timothy 4:7-8*
*1 Corinthians 9:24*
*Hebrews 12:1*

# Safe Harbor

*"God has a way of picking a "nobody"
and turning their world upside down,
in order to create a "somebody"
that will remove the obstacles they
encountered out of the pathway for others."*
Shannon Alde

***Pause and Reflect:*** Having never experienced being on a boat out to sea during a storm, I can only imagine feeling fearful and helpless as forces of nature beyond my control cause great uncertainty. Storms can brew slowly over time or can whip up seemingly out of nowhere and cause great unrest. The ocean is deep and so is our inner life. There can be a huge difference between what's going on far below and on the surface. Deep currents of anxiety, loneliness, uncertainty, and fear can be hidden by a seemingly smooth surface.

We've all experienced life's inner storms. We may experience loss of control or feel battered by our present circumstances. Winds of confusion and discontent swirl around us and we feel trapped in its force. It's time to seek safety and protection.

God is our port in a storm. That's where we find safe harbor. Connecting with God at our most inner core will help us calm the inner currents even as we weather choppy seas.

Why God? Maybe the answer lies in our spiritual ancestor, Jeremiah, who received a message in which God said, "I knew you before I formed you in your mother's womb." There is no depth that God cannot reach. God gets us on levels others may never understand. Our deepest center can be touched, nurtured, comforted and loved by God. Jeremiah endured many storms and much persecution in his life. He listened and found in God a safe port. He embraced his suffering and recognized God had a purpose for his life. Even when we feel battered about by the storms of life, we can call on God to help us use our prior experiences, present instincts, and faith to navigate into safe waters.

***Ponder:*** Whether storms are brewing around you or deep within you, take comfort in knowing that you can turn to God to find safe harbor. Throw out an SOS and be willing to cooperate with God. The answers lie within and will come as you anchor yourself in God. How has God served as a port in the storms of your life? What purpose have the storms of your life served, to help others and yourself navigate choppy waters?

***Pray:*** Dear God, you are my beacon of light in a storm. May I place my complete trust in you as we navigate toward safe harbor.

*Psalm 107: 28-31*
*Isaiah 25: 4-5*
*Deuteronomy 31: 8*

# The Pitter Patter Of Tiny Raindrops

*"You don't think your way into a new kind of living.*
*You live your way into a new kind of thinking."*
Henri Nouwen

***Pause and Reflect:*** We had just returned from an awesome week at a lake in the Adirondacks. The time away with family gave us time to laugh, walk, hike, read, create lovely meals, swim, and kayak. By night, we sat by a blazing fire as a gazillion stars twinkled overhead. No schedules, phone calls, or pressure. Vacation as it is intended to be.

Sitting in my office and answering emails on the first morning back, I suddenly felt overwhelmed with my *to do* list. My mind was reeling. "I have so much preparation to do; how can I possibly get this all together? Where do I begin? The lists are growing; the schedule is tightening!" The pressure was unbearable.

I reminded myself to stop, and ask my body where I was experiencing this pressure. After assessing that it mainly resided in the center of my body, I asked myself to gently take some time to be with the anxious feelings rather than push them away. I took some deep breaths and sat with the feeling of *I'm overwhelmed by it all right now*!

Within a few minutes I became aware of the sound of raindrops tapping on the roof. Gently they fell, just doing what they were meant to do. Gently, they fell, just doing what they were meant to do. Gently they fell, just doing...

Soon the mantra began to permeate my being and the image of the gently falling rain felt right in that moment. I could feel myself calmed by the pitter-patter of the drops upon the roof...upon my heart. Water is an image for hope, quenching my thirst for quiet and peace within. I imagined a tiny stream meandering in the woods. Although I did not see where it began, I trusted it flowed from a powerful source. So, too, the stream that flows inside me is life giving. It will not dry up because its Source is much too caring and giving. Trust. I trusted that all that I needed would be given to me. The raindrops were filling the stream, the stream continued to flow, and I received what I needed.

Calm. A sense of calm returned.

I'm aware that we can be gripped with that same kind of anxiety at any time. We perceive a change, a threat, or anticipate something that hasn't even happened yet. What's the answer? For me it is to stop. Acknowledge the feelings within my body. Allow myself to be with them. I often ask God to place warmth or light directly in the place where I'm feeling the distress in my body. Asking my body if there is a story to be told in the feelings, gives it permission to freely express itself in word, imagery, detail, or whatever.

Rarely does the problem confronting us go away immediately. Speaking for myself, I have lots of planning and writing and creative work in front of me. Nothing changed on the outside. My perception shifted a bit. Rather than the weight of work falling on my shoulders, small raindrops eased gently down. It was a reminder that I can do a little at a time. Instead of feeling stopped up and unable to *think* my way through the next several weeks, I thought of the stream gently meandering within me. It will keep flowing with ideas and words and images that perhaps will be useful as I work. The source will continue to pour forth whatever it is I will need.

What happened the rest of that day? I was inspired to simply clean my cluttered office. Make room. Prepare. Open up space. Clear away the unnecessary. The rest is yet to come. I trust surely it will come.

*Ponder:* For many of us, a change in routine or a transition such as the one I experienced from vacation back to work can cause unrest within. Inevitably, our schedules and calendars fill and change throughout the year. If you find yourself gripped by anxiety or disquiet of any kind, remember to stop, breathe, and ask your body what it needs from you. You may be surprised by the answer! A story, word, feeling, or image may arise amidst the angst that could change your perspective and help you to better navigate your journey.

*Pray:* Dear God, may we find you in the deepest places of our bodies. Tell us the stories you want us to hear, help us to feel the feelings you want us to feel and understand the metaphors and images you create in us.

*Psalm 94:19*
*Matthew 6:34*
*Isaiah 41:13-14*

# July

# May I Have This Dance?

*"The cross is God taking on flesh and blood
and saying, "Me too."*
Rob Bell

***Pause and Reflect:*** I remember the stories they told about you and the things they say you did.

People described you to me in so many different ways. I guess that's because everyone knew you from his or her own experiences.

Do you remember the quiet morning you visited me in the chapel? I closed my eyes to pray and as I gently opened them, there you were beside me. I didn't want to look at you, so I kept my forward gaze. Playfully, I asked you if the image I had of you in my mind was close to the real thing. You smiled and let me know that every unique human image bears your likeness. The rugged GQ image, the compassionate eyes, the tender and loving voice, and your sense of humor are so endearing to me.

It really was love at the first sound of your whispers. Initially, I was so confused. Was this me talking to myself or are You really talking to me? You assured me you were present in all our conversations. Just like your Father spoke to you and just as the Spirit moved in you, so, too, you do that in me.

This kind of love is like a dance. You lead and I follow. As we move it's as if we are one. So closely do we move in an intimate motion that it's barely detectable to those around me on the dance floor we call *life*. And then there are days you want to dance and I sit it out, too busy, not paying attention, wrapped up in my own self. The thing about you is: you never stop asking me to be your partner. Despite your persistence, what I love most about you is that you allow me my space. I'm grateful for all the nudges. Yes, I feel them, but sometimes I'm just not ready to act on them. I can be selfish that way. You give me the freedom to make my own choices. I know there have been plenty of times you could have said, "I told you so" and you didn't. Instead, you are always reassuring me that when I'm ready to dance, you're waiting and ready.

I love the way you take my hand to calm me down. The way you place your hands so gently on my shoulders when I feel the weight of the world on them. I honestly don't know how it happens, but it's as if your strength lifts that extra weight and I feel unburdened. There is an energy in your hands that relaxes my shoulders and I know you'll be with me no matter what's going on in my day. I can't tell you enough how blessed I feel to have you in my life.

Thanks, too, for jogging with me. It's always easier when I can talk with you…it takes my mind off the discomfort. When I'm meeting with people in spiritual direction, I appreciate your presence. On those days when the self-judgment gremlin just doesn't stop yapping at me, thank you for the reminder that I have the option to call on you. I can't thank you enough for the attention you shower on those I love. I'm not sure they always like your plans, but I see that they are talking with you more often…that warms my heart.

I don't know of anyone else who would stay up at night, and, while I sleep, keep vigil over me, protect me, and continue loving me into my deepest rest. And you've promised to stay with me until my last breath and beyond.

You are the Friend I try to introduce to everyone. I think they all really like you, but they need to get to know you better. But you know how that goes…. after all these years, we're still working at our relationship. It takes what it takes.

I'm just waking up, Dear Friend; I look forward to talking with you today. And please remember all those people who are feeling lonely, angry, hurt, prideful, and arrogant. Today may be the day they want to dance. If you need me to meet them, give me the strength and courage to be present to them.

*Ponder:* The dance floor is open; are you willing to dance?

*Pray:* Dear God, sometimes I hear you in a whisper or feel you like a flutter deep inside. Sometimes, I taste you in nature's salty air and sea. But it is when I see your presence in others, and sense your presence beside me, that I truly am at peace.

*Exodus 33:14*
*Jeremiah 29:13*
*1 John 4:12*

# Silent Support

*"The friend who can be silent with us*
*in a moment of despair or confusion,*
*who can stay with us*
*in an hour of grief and bereavement,*
*who can tolerate not knowing...*
*not healing, not curing...*
*that is a friend who cares."*
Henri Nouwen

***Pause and Reflect:*** There are certainly times when an arm around the shoulder, a hand placed over another hand, a hug, or word of support is necessary for someone who is experiencing inner turmoil.

However, sometimes, it is best to allow the person their space and offer silent support in their presence. Silent support is sacred attention.

Have you been in a situation when a vulnerable person begins to share something from within, and emotions overtake them? Tears begin to flow or the person becomes silently adrift in their own turmoil. They have something important to say, but are finding it difficult to articulate the words. Have you also been present when someone breaks the silence or the flow by rushing for a tissue box, placing an arm around the person, or speaking up so as to rescue the person from his or her difficulty? This may be a well-intentioned response that often has the effect of closing down the personal expression of emotions.

It's important to remember that it's often in the silence that breakthroughs are possible. Not trying to fix someone can be the most loving response we can make toward another person. While it may feel awkward and uncomfortable to us, silence is a golden opportunity for growth. Simply put, remaining present and allowing the person to let go of the pent-up feelings is spiritual therapy. Allowing others to fully experience sincere emotions is a gift you can give to another.

There is usually plenty of time after the emotions have surfaced and settled into sacred space to offer physical or emotional support. The opportunity to offer silent support may be fleeting and yet so important.

**Ponder:** Awareness of your own emotions is key. Settle yourself. Allow the silence to go undisturbed. Ask God for the wisdom to know when silent support is far more precious than advice or the desire to fix it. Recall a situation in which you were present to someone who was vulnerable, grieving, or despairing. Looking back, was there anything you learned about your response that will help you in the future? How does it feel for you to be silent with another person experiencing emotions that are challenging?

**Pray:** Dear God, help me to offer silent support to others. May my ears listen and receive with compassion and love.

*James 1:19*
*Proverbs 2:2*
*Mark 4:24*

# Chance Encounter

*" To every soul you encounter,
be a mirror, which reflects only their beauty."*
Bryant McGill

***Pause and Reflect:*** Is there someone with whom you've had a chance meeting, someone who has changed your life for the better?

I met a friend for life while I was in school. This friendship didn't start up in a classroom, in the cafeteria, or in the halls of the school, but rather in the gym, at a basketball game.

He came to my hometown from New York City in 1912 when he was twelve years old. He worked his entire life as a farmer on the outskirts of our town. One of his passions was watching high school basketball. Both Arthur and I were seniors - he seasoned with age and wisdom, and I in high school.

One day as I waited for my sister's basketball game to begin, an older gentleman approached and asked me if I had a schedule handy for the winter sports season. I told him I did not, but would be glad to pick one up for him and bring it to the next home game. It would have been easy to blow off this request; however, there was something about this gentle man I just could not forget.

I retrieved a schedule from the office and carried it with me to the next game.

I saw the old man come into the gym and find a seat in the bleachers. I pulled out the schedule, ran down the steps, and sat down beside him. I presented him with the schedule and we introduced ourselves to one another. We talked about the upcoming season and the girls' chances of winning the tournament. After our conversation I returned to my seat and watched the game. A quick wave good-bye at the end of the game and our brief encounter seemed like history.

Instead, Arthur sent a beautiful note to my home address thanking me for remembering to bring the sports schedule. To me, this simple act certainly didn't warrant such a response. To Arthur, any act of kindness was an opportunity for him to express his gratitude.

I was touched by his response and made it a point to spend a little time with Arthur before every game he attended. We talked about family, the farm, his love of gardening, his childhood…whatever! A wonderful friendship blossomed.

Every summer I received complimentary tickets to the hometown fair. Arthur was so proud of his flower arrangements, decorated gourds, and the mobiles he created of his "famous friends", pictures of movie stars with the name of the local friend who he thought resembled the star. He was a fixture at the fair and everyone knew him. His invitation to the farm for homemade ice cream and a tour of the gardens was answered enthusiastically. I know I wasn't the only person whose life was touched by this gracious man, although he had a way of making me feel like the most special friend in the world.

Birthday cards, graduation cards, letters of support, updates, pictures and articles went back and forth for many years, until at last he could no longer write.

I knew nothing about Arthur's religion, or if he even practiced a faith. Arthur was all about love. He lived his spirituality. He reveled in the simple beauty of nature and humanity. Everyone was treated with respect and dignity. Arthur was a master in the art of joy making.

I have a picture and an article that I've kept for years about my friend. I'm so grateful for that chance meeting that led to years of friendship. Arthur died several years ago at age of ninety-three. I will always remember him fondly, with a smile and a few tears in my eyes.

***Ponder:*** Today, think back to a chance encounter that positively affected your life. Choose to celebrate your past chance encounters and open your heart and mind to all the future chance encounters coming your way! Who knows? Today could be that day! How might you honor someone from your past that has been a true light in your life? Say a prayer for them, send a note of gratitude, share a story about the person or perform a random act of kindness, keeping them in mind.

*Pray:* Dear God, thank you for chance encounters that bring wonderful people into my life. May I keep an open mind and heart, so if by chance, an opportunity comes my way to meet someone new, I'm ready to receive them as I would a friend of many years.

*Matthew 10:29*
*Luke 10:31*
*Romans 8:28*

# Summer Blooms

*"There is a fruitfulness about your life
that you've not fully discovered.
Implant your roots deep into your heart's good soil
where a treasure of nourishment waits for you."*
Macrina Wiederkehr

***Pause and Reflect:*** Lilies, columbine, ferns, butterfly bushes, boxwoods, asters, solomon's plume and Russian sage are among the flowers and shrubs growing in my gardens. Each grows in its own place and blooms in its own time. Each plant makes the garden look beautiful. They are attractive for different reasons; the stems, shape, flowers, fragrance and color.

The gardens that come to life each spring and summer in our yards teach us a lot about the "garden of life."

Our lives mirror the cycle of life we see in a garden.

The seeds wait deep beneath the surface until the earth warms and they've had time to mature. So, too, do our dreams and ideas need time to develop, so as to be fruitful for the world when they are ready to bloom.

The green stems reaching out for sun and rain enjoy being nurtured by the life-giving source. God will provide everything necessary to help us nurture those dreams. Our responsibility is to reach out and receive the positive energy and grace that comes through the circumstances and people placed in our path.

Buds wrapped tight within themselves remain protected until they can risk opening themselves up to the waiting world. Most often, it is best not to force things to happen, but rather, to move when we feel the Spirit nudging us onward.

And when a plant blooms it adds its most unique gifts to the garden. Placing our trust in the Master Gardener helps us to risk becoming the unique person

God intends us to be.

Sometimes weeds encroach on a vibrant plant and threaten its health. There may be times when outside distractions challenge our well being. We must surround ourselves with people whose positive energy uplifts us and helps us to mature and grow.

*Ponder:* Blooming, withering, dying and rebirth are the natural cycle of a garden. So too, every idea and dream has a cycle. We celebrate. We love. We grow. And hopefully, we learn to accept that sometimes we need to let go in order for something new to be brought forth. What is blooming within you at this time that needs to be nurtured? What is withering and needs to be let go?

*Pray:* Dear God, thank you for all that blooms in my garden. Help me to continue weeding, and tending to my inner garden through every season of life.

*Matthew 6:26-30*
*John 15:16*
*Luke 8:11*

# Leap of Faith

*"If we never had the courage to take a leap of faith,*
*we'd be cheating God out of a chance to*
*mount us up with wings like eagles*
*and watch us soar."*
Jen Stephens

***Pause and Reflect:*** Taking a leap of faith compels us to commit to a deeply held belief, idea, or dream while trusting in something greater than ourselves to help us move with the experience.

It doesn't mean we are free of fear but rather that the fear does not incapacitate us. Placing our faith in God, we are able to tune inward and come up with an answer that is based on what we feel is right, good, and just. By listening to our gut instincts we are moved by the Spirit to make choices based on God's deepest desires for us. Trusting our intuition we move with tolerance, understanding, compassion and openness.

For example, I took a leap of faith in deciding to leave a job I truly enjoyed. After a year of discernment I felt nudged by the Spirit to a ministry that required more flexibility in my schedule. The pull became so strong I could no longer deny my desire to explore the ideas floating around inside of me.

Yes, there was fear and doubt. I asked myself if I was crazy to give up my work, a steady paycheck, and a certain comfort level that came with years of experience. I chose to trust that God would provide whatever experiences were necessary for me to move toward a new dream. When I left my job, I had a few dreams, the support of family and friends and my faith in God.

I've been reminded over and over again that God never said it would be easy. That *leap of faith* has changed my life in so many ways. It has meant the difference between living in the relative safety of things I know and taking risks with things I've yet to learn. Faith in God provides new opportunities for growth emotional and spiritual growth. I'm learning to cherish times of stillness, rather than constantly moving. Yes, life still has its bumpy moments, but God is giving me the strength to move through those times and learn something from them.

*Ponder:* Today, pray for the courage to open up the floodgates to the God-given potential within you. Let the expectations go. Turn it over to God and allow yourself to trust the process by which you are being led. Let God surprise you! Is there something in your life calling you to take a leap of faith? What is holding you back? What do you need to take a step forward?

*Pray:* Dear God, help me to discern your will. Let me clearly see what is holding me back from being all that you want me to be.

*Philippians 4: 13-14*
*Matthew 14: 28-31*
*1 Samuel 17: 45-46*

# Deep Into the Actual

*"To take what there is,
and use it without waiting forever in vain
for the preconceived-
to dig deep into the actual and
get something out of that-
this doubtless is the way to live."*
Henry James

***Pause and Reflect:*** I don't want to waste time in the what if's or should be's. What is before me is part of my process. I may not see the big picture and therefore have many questions. Questions are good. Ultimately I must trust that God will lead me through whatever is my present reality. If I choose to live for the someday when... I miss out on what is right here now. There are so many lessons to learn in the present; why rush? When the present reality feels uncomfortable it's easy to want out! I have to remind myself that God is in the discomfort as well.

Presence is about paying attention to the Spirit's movement in me as I am being moved. Ah...and the kicker...what about those times I'm not feeling especially moved...can I be in that space for awhile, trusting that is my *actual*? Can I live with the questions and prayers until an answer comes?

Every morning that we rise is an opportunity to face a new, sometimes challenging day. We won't always have the answers. It doesn't mean we give up on new ideas or problem- solving. We may have to dig a little deeper. We may have to let go and begin again. What is there presently may have to be sufficient until something new presents itself.

God revels in our ability to use our instincts, brains, and gut feelings to discern the questions of our present reality. After all, it is God who gifted us with these abilities and gives us the freedom to choose. It is important to direct our prayer toward God in order that we may receive the wisdom to choose wisely. We don't have to go it alone!

Accepting our reality actually allows us to move forward. It frees us from worn out thoughts and patterns that may not serve us in the present. It allows us to accept the truth and to open our eyes to new potential and new possibilities.

***Ponder:*** Today, rather than focusing on things that cannot be changed or looking ahead in worry, allow yourself some time to pray into your reality. Listen and notice where the Spirit is leading you. What is God revealing to you today that needs your attention? What may help you focus in on the present moments of this day?

***Pray:*** Dear God, help me to live into what is before me, and trust that all the answers I need to know will be given to me in your time.

*Habakkuk 2:3*
*Proverbs 3:5-6*
*2 Peter 3:8*

# August

# Retreat And Engage

*"A good balance between
masculine and feminine energy
is to balance your life
between retreats and confronts.
Make sure you do pull back and reflect
in your solitude or in your prayers,
but make sure also that there is some
engagement, involvement, incarnation,
some activity."*
Richard Rohr

***Ponder and Reflect:*** While retreating is essential to one's wholeness, it doesn't necessarily make one holy.

Since retreat work, spiritual companioning, religious education and spiritual programs are the focus of my ministry, it helps to step back often and ask myself, "so just how are *you* serving others as you *preach*? Rohr contends that there is no more effective way to run from God than to talk the talk without walking the walk. Thus, the question I ask myself is so important.

In previous reflections, I've warned about spiritual snobbery. It's easy to get caught up in the idea that because someone reads the newest and latest and greatest spiritual authors, or attends religious services regularly, or is involved in some new and enlightened ideas, that somehow they have the better line to God. All these things turned inward only for the purpose of self-fulfillment may leave us no closer to God. And often they may find us repeating an old favorite line, "Is that all there is?"

Without practice, without service to our fellow men and women, these pious and holy retreats leave an empty feeling inside of us. But here's the good news: if you are feeling empty, feeling as though there is something missing, or feeling out of balance, trust those feelings to move you toward God's call. Pay attention to that emptiness. Being empty is not such a bad thing. It's in the emptiness that we can pay attention to God's voice and urgings. This is where dark areas become filled with light. Avoid the temptation to fill that space with more stuff for yourself. Instead, ask God what service you are called forth to give. Imagine an empty bucket being poured out, refilled, and poured out once again. That's how it is with God. We are empty and being filled and poured out daily. That's the incarnation.

A priest was retelling a story that had been passed on to him from a teacher in seminary. The teacher was describing the fundamental role of the prophets, priests, and therefore all Christians. "We are called," he said, "as Jesus reminds us, to comfort the afflicted." He then added, "We are also called to afflict the comfortable." The lesson: we must by our actions invite those who remain in their comfort zones to join us in action. To follow Jesus we must go to places that are not always comfortable. We must challenge others and ourselves to reach out beyond what always feels *safe*.

***Ponder:*** How am I bringing peace, comfort, compassion, tolerance, and love to those in my corner of the world? It's not always an easy thing to do. The challenge is for us to stretch out beyond our comfy spaces. How can we make a difference in someone's life today? How does our light shine in the darkness of another's space?

***Pray:*** Dear God, I ask for the wisdom to know day-to-day, when it's time to retreat and when it's time to serve. Lead me toward you through serving others.

*1 Peter 4:10-11*
*John 13:12-14*
*1 John 3:18*

# Discovering The Divine In Our Losses

*"I lie in my hospital room and moan.
A tidal wave has swept over me and
I am trying to hold it back with my bare hand.
I cry from so deep inside of me...
deeper than I've ever known.
I cry because my hand is so small
and the wave so powerful.
I am not strong enough.
I am at the bottom of a black pit,
and I don't care."*

Paula D'Arcy

***Pause and Reflect:*** Our encounters with the Divine range from moments of joyful awe to the deepest loss imaginable. D'Arcy's book is a personal memoir. She discovers God in places she never expected. After the tragic loss of her daughter and husband in a car accident, caused by a drunk driver, she finds herself struggling to even want to live.

If you have aging parents, a family member with mental illness or physical challenges, if you are dealing with addictions, death, the loss of employment or a relationship, or for any reason are feeling broken, you may relate to the feelings of the *black pit*.

For Christians, we come to understand our own brokenness by the Cross. Our capacities to hope, heal, and love more deeply are dependent on our faith. It's not necessarily our intellectual knowledge of religious doctrine, but rather our heartfelt responses and surrender to God that offers us a glimpse of restoration or a return to wholeness.

Sometimes the *black pit*, although extremely uncomfortable, is where we learn to surrender. We realize that old ways of doing things don't work. Perhaps we understand that nothing could have prepared us for the depth of feelings we are experiencing. All the wealth, pleasure, honor, and power we once thought filled us up inside no longer matter. Maybe you've discovered that all the best-laid plans have left you feeling frustrated and disillusioned.

After all, what is it that we fear about the darkness? The not knowing, the inability to see clearly? Is it that we feel we don't deserve joy, or that change of any kind may be worse than complacency?

An experience of the *black pit* may leave us feeling out of control, desperate, numb, apathetic, confused, sad, or lonely amongst other emotions. God's Light gives us a glimmer of hope.

We desire it.

We search for it.

We abandon our intellect, senses, and emotions to something greater than ourselves.

Past solutions don't necessarily light a spark within us. We may not know this God of Mystery, but we've heard others speak about this Light. We are encouraged to trust the way of those who have experienced the Light.

Is it the blind leading the blind? The answer in a sense is yes. Those who have been touched by God in their own blindness and now see differently can help those who need to see with a new set of eyes. Those who live in the Light know the experience of trusting the God of Mystery. It is in the deepest depths of despair that we can learn to let go and trust in something Greater than ourselves. It is a personal choice.

*Ponder:* We need not attempt to force change. This may sound crazy, but often, before we can begin to heal, we must embrace the darkness. Own it as a part of us. Feel it. Be present to it. With God's presence in it we allow it to yield up its gift. There's only one direction one can choose to go from the black pit—toward the Light. Allow God to hold you, show you, and place others in your life to help you see with a new set of eyes. It is a new vision with a heartfelt sense of trust and willingness in the Divine.

*Pray:* Dear God, as we search for you, may we feel the surge of light welling up deep inside of us. May we always move toward the One True Light that warms the interior of our being.

*John 8:12*
*Psalm 119:105*
*John 12:35*

# Crossroads

*"Often we stand at life's crossroads and*
*view what we think is the end...*
*but God has much bigger vision and*
*He tells us...relax my child, it's only a bend."*
Zeeshan Saltar

***Pause and Reflect:*** You've heard the familiar expression, "I'm at a crossroad." We can visualize coming to a four-way stop at an intersection. There is a short pause before we determine which road or direction we should take to continue on our journey. If the intersection is one that is familiar to us, and we're in a rush to reach our destination, we may choose the quicker path. Other times, we might choose the longer, more scenic route. When faced with an unfamiliar intersection, in a place we've never been, our pause may be just a little longer or more cautious.

In real life, sometimes we come to a crossroad and we are unsure of which way to turn. In that moment of decision, it may be the pause that makes a difference. In the pauses of life, we can take time to look back. What past experiences have served to bring us to this present place? What successes and failures have shaped us? What might we need to let go of to move forward? In deciding where we're going, it's important to place God in charge of the directions. It doesn't mean we won't lose our way occasionally, or that the ride will always be smooth, but rather, that we have a guide to help us navigate the journey. Don't we always feel safer traveling with a companion, a co-pilot of sorts?

When we invite God into the pause, our mind is released of fear, panic, or judgment. We make a decision to trust the movement of the Spirit to help guide us. We open ourselves to the possibilities that may lie ahead in every direction. We trust our inner compass so long as we've put God in charge.

***Ponder:*** As you meander through your day and come to a crossroad, be aware of the pause. Invite God into your consciousness and take the path that makes sense to you. The road may be a straight shot to your destination or have a few twists and turns along the way. Let the Spirit be your GPS! Stop. Pause. Notice. Listen. Decide. Go with it! Describe a crossroad you have come to in your life. Describe the decisions you've had to make. What did you learn about others, God, and yourself? How will this experience help you in navigating the journey ahead?

*Pray:* Dear God, I trust you to help me navigate through this day. Help me to trust my inner GPS so that I may do your will in all things.

*Psalm 25: 4-5*
*Numbers 14: 8-9*
*John 16:13*

# It's About Your Passion, Not Your Position

*"Desire that your life count for something great!*
*Long for your life to have eternal significance.*
*Want this! Don't coast through life without a passion."*
John Piper

***Pause and Reflect:*** The origin of the word passion centers on Christ's suffering leading up to and including His ultimate death on the cross. In his suffering Jesus' purpose was fulfilled, to do his Father's will and to atone for our sins. Clearly, Jesus endured his passion in order to serve others. In fulfilling his passion, Jesus did not seek, nor use, prestige, possessions, or power to save himself. Rather, "he emptied himself." (Philippians 2:7)

Today we use the word passion to describe feelings. Passion comes from a place deep within us. It is something that stirs us up, so much so, that we feel like we'll burst at the seams if we aren't following our desire. We come alive whenever we feel the presence of this desire. There are times our passion brings great joy. Sometimes our passions arise out of painful circumstances. Passion draws us out of complacency, and moves us toward something with vigor. When God is at the core of our passions we are pulled toward something that is life-giving.

Talent, prestige, and position have nothing to do with passion. Achievement is wonderful; however, we must see it as gift from God. Passion may begin with an interest in something or a willingness to learn; a child develops a passion for a musical instrument. It may be in response to something that touches our soul. A loving parent is passionate about helping a child who is struggling. Our passion may be intermingled with suffering. Saint Mother Teresa's passion for the poor and dying in the slums of Calcutta must have been a double-edged sword of joy and suffering.

Our passion may give insight into God's purpose for us. When God inspires us, it is clear that our passion is meant to be of service to others. Passion that is not shared withers. This God-centered passion doesn't necessarily mean a person is oozing with emotion. Passion manifests itself in many forms: in prayer, creativity, good works, meditation, activity, learning, or contemplation. We find ourselves open and willing to receive whatever it is God intends for us.

**Ponder:** It's amazing what can happen in our lives when we immerse ourselves in the love of Christ, and open our hearts and minds to learning from the circumstances and experiences before us. Pay attention to your desires. Ask God to guide them. See where your passion takes you. Think about times you have felt passion well up inside of you. Go deeper. What is it you truly desired?

**Pray:** Dear God, help me to align my desires with your desires for me. May every desire of my soul serve you in thought, word, and deed.

*John 14:12*
*Psalms 32:8*
*Colossians 3:23*

# My God Is Wrapped In Skin

*"Few things communicate acceptance and warmth*
*to us as much as touch.*
*Even a child knows its value.*
*One night a mother went into her little girl's bedroom*
*to comfort her in the midst of a thunderstorm.*
*The mother said,*
*"Don't worry, Jesus is here and he will protect you."*
*Her daughter responded,*
*"Okay, you sleep here with Jesus and I will go to sleep*
*with Daddy!"*
*That child wanted touch!"*

Gayle D. Erwin

**Pause and Reflect:** We see the power of physical touch in scripture stories. The woman who is suffering from hemorrhage and considered unclean by her peers touches Jesus' cloak and is healed because of her faith. Jesus touched the man with leprosy and healed him. He healed a blind man by spitting on and touching his eyes. And when Thomas doubted his resurrection, Jesus told him to place his fingers into his side. We can almost hear the words, "C'mon Thomas, put those fingers right into this wound. It's real; I'm real. And I did what I told you I would do."

Perhaps photographer Dewitt Jones in his video *Celebrate What's Right with the World*, explained it best, "Most of us say, ' "I won't believe it until I see it. Perhaps we have it wrong. More than likely, we won't see it until we believe it.' "

What a gift believers have been given...our God came with skin on. Born in a humble stable, in a pretty unpopular town, the "bastard" child of two rather ordinary people, of a lineage that included womanizers, prostitutes, adulterers, and murderers. Growing up couldn't have been easy. According to Isaiah, his looks were nothing to desire. He hung out in the temple area talking with old men; even those closest to him found his teachings confounding at times. And speaking of his choice of "homies," they really were a sad lot: fishermen, tax collectors, a political zealot, and a few tradesmen. They were

146

hardly on the A-list.

I have to believe that God, who could have shown his power and might in any way possible, knew that we needed to be touched physically as well as emotionally and spiritually.

Jesus is above all else relatable. He understood vulnerability in every way possible. He touched others and allowed himself to be touched. He understood joy, loneliness, fear, anger, sadness, confusion, and all the other feelings we experience as human beings. God made us in his image and likeness so that we could, like Jesus, comfort others, listen, learn to forgive, extend kindnesses, and to help others heal with whatever power comes through us from God.

*Ponder:* When we're in a vulnerable place, we need one another's touch. We need real ears to hear our story. It's important to feel the presence of another, even when all we need is a good cry and nothing else needs to be said. The importance of a hug can never be overrated. The touch of someone's hand over ours is so reassuring.

Notice the times that you are touched by someone this week. Pay attention to how you touch others. Ask yourself how God is present in those moments for you. How does touch make a difference in your day-to-day experiences?

*Pray:* Dear God, thank you for sending your Son into our world. It is through him that we more fully understand what it means to show compassion, empathy, warmth, understanding and love. Help us to reach out to those in need of our touch this day.

*Daniel 10:18*
*Mark 10:16*
*Matthew 9:29*

# Realize Not Analyze

*"If we think about it,*
*if we begin to analyze it,*
*if we start to argue with it*
*or try to 'figure it out,'*
*we'll become lost in thought."*
Neale Walsch

***Pause and Reflect:*** While on a retreat in Narragansett, R.I., I got up early one morning before the sunrise, and went for a walk along the beach. Initially, I could only see shadows of objects because of the early morning darkness. Soon streaks of blue, orange, purple, yellow, and red lined the horizon. It was a glorious transformation and I was excited to welcome the sunrise. My eyes were fixed eastward. The clouds, the colors, the water were ablaze in beauty!

As I watched, my body began to respond to this scene before me. I felt calm and yet giddy. My heart felt full and my mind raced with thoughts. How could it be that I was feeling this conflict within myself? I wanted to take it all in and just be, but my mind began to wander. What am I feeling? How can I describe this feeling? If I were to write a reflection on this moment, what would I say? My work mind was beginning to take over and I was fully aware of it.

Before leaving the house for the beach, I had grabbed a book for meditation. It was Eckhart Tolle's book, *Stillness Speaks*, which I had never read and had no familiarity with whatsoever. I sat down in the sand and opened the book. The sun was now a bright, magnificent, orange, glowing ball. I had no other intention except to open the book and read a passage with which to meditate.

I cannot quote exactly what I read, but the point that hit home in that moment was that sometimes we have to stop analyzing and just be. BINGO! I read one paragraph and closed the book. Message received. Rather than allowing this moment to wash over me, I was trying to work every angle of this experience in my head.

It's not always easy for us to shut off our working minds. We can become distracted in the stillness. I tried to let it all go and just be, but it seemed that distraction won out on this morning. It was still a beautiful experience and yet, I realized something seemed lost.

I shared this experience with the group of people on retreat with me. I wondered aloud, how often in the course of a day do I neglect the opportunity to "just be" with an experience, rather than analyze it? How often do I glance and "get busy" rather than linger in a moment? Analyzing and presence seem at odds with one another. Both have a place in our day and yet, I'm not so sure how necessary the former was in watching a sunrise.

As I sat to write my thoughts down in a journal, I did not have the Tolle book with me and therefore could not quote what I had read that morning on the beach. I found instead an author's review of the book. I kid you not; this was a line in his review: "Trying to analyze a sunrise, the experience will go away." I can't make this up! I suppose my self-analysis of the entire event was spot on.

**Ponder:** Maybe next time I watch a sunrise, I'll remind myself to "just be" attentive to the rising sun and leave the work behind. Perhaps then, the experience will be of the senses and the heart rather than simply of the mind. The greater lesson is that within the course of our days there is more opportunity for presence and lingering. We can pray that our capacity to experience both increases.

**Pray:** Dear God, help me to pay attention to the little things that matter. Let my sense of awe and wonder come alive as I experience your presence in the bounty of this day.

*Psalm: 72:16*
*Deuteronomy 28:12*
*2 Corinthians 9:8*

# September

# An Outside-In Day

*"Distractions become prayers when we keep with God.
However, resisting them can make us more distracted."*
Madeleine Delbrel

***Pause and Reflect:*** We've all experienced those days when we're inside wishing we could be outside. And, then there are days we are outside pining for a cup of tea, a good book, and a comfy chair inside.

On this particular morning I had an *inside* to-do list and asked God to help me find the willingness to get it done. With upcoming retreats and programs, the planning and preparation seemed endless. As I was doing my morning exercises, my mind wandered to the outside. Shrubs needed trimming, gardens needed weeding, decks needed cleaning, and fall plants needed planting. The outside was looking pretty inviting! With the *inside* to-do list still on my mind, I was having a difficult time deciding what my focus should be.

As often happens, I decided to check my insides. What's my body telling me? What feels right for this day? I soon found myself grabbing rakes, shovels, and trimming equipment. A perfect late summer day filled with sunshine, warmth, and a gentle breeze. I began to concentrate on one small job after another. My senses were alive. I noticed the smell of the morning air and felt the gentle breeze on my face. I felt gratitude for summer months awash in the most delightful weather imaginable. As my hands played in the soil and my body worked itself into a feel-good ache, I reveled in the results.

Surprisingly, something else was happening as I worked in the yard. My mind began to fill with ideas to help me with my inside work. Inspiration was coming from every direction. After many hours and much work completed outside, I came inside to write. Creative thoughts were flowing; my head was clear, and soon pages were filled with little bits of wisdom inspired by the Holy Spirit.

***Ponder:*** Our spiritual journey is an inside-outside experience as well. We must pay attention to God's presence in the people, places, and experiences going on around us as well as our internal responses to those very things.

There are days when the outside world can be demanding, challenging, loud, and overstimulating. It is then that we crave quiet time to pray and to just be alone with God. It is in this space that we can listen to the whispers of the Spirit. We can muster strength and courage. The quiet allows us time to reflect on questions we've been meaning to ask ourselves or perhaps are avoiding. It is in the quiet of the inside that we find renewal and inspiration.

So, too, there are times when we need to get outside ourselves and into action. Working with or for others, or in nature provides the perfect diversion for filling us up. God always has a purpose for our being, giving, serving, and loving in this world.

I was grateful for my outside-in day! Once again, I was able to experience the lesson of one of my mentors, Sr. Florence. She would often say, "there's only a one letter difference between play and pray." Sometimes we need to just get outside and play! What happens in the playing is that our prayers are heard. Our minds open and we become filled with creativity and hope.

Pray: Dear God, I pray that today we will experience balance in caring for our insides and outsides. May we be inspired by the Holy Spirit and grateful for all the gifts that come our way as the result of our efforts and God's amazing grace.

*Jeremiah 31:4*
*Matthew 6:21*
*Romans 12:2*

# Taking Care Of Unfinished Business

*"I learned a long time ago*
*that some people would rather die than forgive.*
*It's a strange truth,*
*but forgiveness is a painful and difficult process.*
*It's not something that happens overnight.*
*It's an evolution of the heart."*
Sue Monk Kidd

***Pause and Reflect:*** There are plenty of opportunities in our life just waiting for an open and willing heart to receive them. Sometimes our hearts are bound in chains holding us to the past. Before we can be completely set free from our own prisons, we must address unfinished business from our past.

When a trust has been broken within a relationship, family, or friendship, it often takes time for healing and communication to resume. Sometimes our wanting to move forward or get on with things causes us to move too soon and people may get hurt. So what do we do when we know there is unfinished business from our past?

Far be it from me to have all the answers on forgiveness, but here is what I'm learning:

No one is exempt from doing wrong. Therefore, we need to take time to examine any bitterness, anger, or resentment that resides in our own heart. It may sound crazy, but rather than dismiss it, we can learn to embrace it. Listen deep within, and see if there is a story that needs to unfold from the feelings. We ask God to take away anything that blocks us from forgiving. This may take repeated attempts, but over time we feel a shift in our attitude and disposition.

Pray for the person or people involved. Prayer is a powerful tool in setting our hearts in the right direction, toward God's will for us.

Remember the words, "love is patient; love is kind." There is no guarantee others will accept any offerings we make toward restitution or reconciliation. By loving, we are not trying to *fix* anyone. We are simply doing the right thing. In doing the right thing the chains loosen and our hearts are set free. When judgment of others enters our minds, as it often does when we are hurting, we simply become aware of it, and ask that our thoughts become aligned with God's will for us. It takes practice and perseverance. God can shine a light in our darkness. This light can change even a hardened heart.

If our actions have caused pain we need to own it. There is no exemption from responsibility for the consequences of our past behavior. Even when God forgives us, there is still an expectation that we make restitution.

*Ponder:* Jesus was an amazing role model for us. Free of the chains of power, prestige, or possessions, even when nailed to the cross, he chose forgiveness as one of his last acts of humanity. Are you ready to set the prisoner free? Are your minds and hearts willing to turn to God, to help you take care of some unfinished business?

*Pray:* Dear God, free me from the bondage of self. Today, open my heart, mind, and desires to your will for me.

*Galatians 5:1*
*2 Corinthians 3:17*
*1 Peter 2:16*

# Facing Fears

*"Fear has two meanings:*
*Forget Everything And Run or*
*Face Everything And Rise.*
*The Choice is Yours."*
Zig Ziglar

**Pause and Reflect:** I decided to take some time away from weekly writing and painting in order to focus on some new ideas and plans percolating within me. Those new ideas were specifically intended to support my burning passion to continue helping others to build relationships with one another and God. Free of deadlines and worry, I had plenty of time to...well...get sidetracked again!

I had every intention of updating my website and getting a short video made explaining my book and mission. You know what they say about the best-laid plans. However, I did not let fear of failure, fear of the unknown, or fear of the best laid plans stop me from letting God do what God does best: lead me.

During the hiatus I asked people for help with a special project. Twelve times I gathered a group of people for prayer, to do some group focusing, a little journaling, and to share our experiences with one another. What came out of these sessions was a new appreciation for the power of vulnerability, faith, and wisdom.

Before the hiatus began, my thoughts were wandering toward a second book. I could feel the fear creeping in. Thoughts of sleepless nights, publishing deadlines, constant second-guessing, rewrites, and the like could have easily paralyzed me. I shared my thoughts with only a handful of people. One morning I was talking with my husband and I heard exactly what I needed to hear. After listening into my deepest anxieties he said, "You don't need to write a book, just write to write."

Was it possible? To write, just to write? To write, just for the joy of writing? Oh God, why must I make things so complicated? Of course, I could write...

just to write. I began writing and it was like a faucet had been turned on. I didn't want to stop. Day and night, on and off, I wrote. Then, the idea of working with the groups added to the excitement of my writing.

The result was that my little project looks like a second book. God truly is amazing. I was led down another path during my hiatus. It was leading me toward my passion; it just did not look like I envisioned it would be. It was enjoyable, loose, powerful, and fearless. This is a great example of what happens when we let go of our plans and let God do his work with us. We need only to let God surprise us!

*Ponder:* God-willing, we will be able to face any fears that come up and push through them, not for vainglory, but rather, to honor the creative stirrings of the Spirit. We may experience incredibly wonderful periods of self-discovery. What burning desire am I willing to turn over to God? What may help me pay attention to God's unfolding plans for me?

*Pray:* Dear God, may all my desires come before you and be centered in you. Take my fears and teach me to accept and to live into your plans, so that I may always know your will. Whatever unfolds, help me to trust that it will be in service, thanksgiving, and praise to you and others.

*Isaiah 41:10*
*Romans 8:15*
*Psalm 56: 3-4*

# Fall Revelations

*"Autumn is a second spring*
*where every leaf is a flower."*
Albert Camus

**Pause and Reflect:** As a New Englander, I've always appreciated the gift of observing changes in nature in a rather brilliant and obvious way. The leaves on the trees change dramatically from greens to yellows, oranges, and reds. The day's light grows shorter and the nights become much cooler. A blanket of frost covers the morning landscape and leaves begin to fall in the blustery winds. The fields yield the bounty of the last harvest of the season. Animals scamper in search of food to sustain them through a harsh winter.

My home is nestled inside a hill and surrounded by nature's beauty. There are thousands of trees, rock formations, and, to the west, deep within the woods, a naturally running stream with a waterfall.

During the summer when the foliage is rich and green, it is impossible to see the water. As the leaves begin to turn color, decay, and eventually fall to the earth, the woods become stark. Through the barren trees a running brook and waterfall is revealed.

I remember the first fall season we spent in our home. Being unfamiliar with the layout of the land, I was surprised to see the waterfall for the first time. It was as if a story was unfolding before me of what had been hidden deep in the woods.

Sometimes, in our personal lives, things need to be shed in order that other wonderful things are revealed to us. The autumn season of our inner lives provides much the same opportunity as the natural outer season. It is a transitional time, a movement, ever so slightly toward change.

**Ponder:** As we become aware of the seasonal changes, we keep our eyes and heart open wide. We alert our senses to what may be dying inside of us, in order that something new may be revealed. We let go of the unimportant things in order to let God reveal to us those things that nurture our spirits. Rather than forcing things to happen, we let nature take its course and revel in its bounty and surprise. Absolutes, shoulds, restlessness, and superficiality are examined through the eyes of wisdom. We learn to bend. It's OK to say maybe or maybe not. We manage to sit with our stirrings, whatever they may be. And, we begin to go deep inside to depths never imagined. What has been hidden for many seasons is slowly revealed within. What has been revealed to you that perhaps has come as a surprise? How did it change you in any way?

***Pray:*** Dear God, as the seasons naturally change, may I be mindful always of the inner conversions and transitions that lead me toward your love and grace.

*Hebrews 13: 8*
*Genesis 8:22*
*Ecclesiastes 3:1*

# Retreating

*"Jesus was a hiker.*
*The wilderness was His retreat."*
Toni Sorenson

**Pause and Reflect:** I attended a business meeting at a local retreat center. The question asked of the group was, "What makes this place special?" Without any hesitation, a gentleman spoke up. "This place saved my life." He went on to talk about a time earlier in his life when he was down and out and the bottle was his only friend. Someone invited him on a retreat. He said he felt like he was in the home of a trusting and loving friend when he entered the retreat house. Everyone accepted him just as he was. Over the course of the weekend retreat he discovered he had the potential for a whole new relationship with God. No longer was it alcohol, but his newfound spirituality that filled him to the brim.

That same evening at another retreat center, I had the opportunity to welcome women, many for whom this was their first weekend retreat experience. It took nothing more than a simple hug and welcome at the front door before the shoulders softened and the smiles brightened. After the evening prayer service, one by one, those seasoned with years of retreat experience made newcomers feel right at home with stories, experiences, and savory home baked goodies to share.

I wonder why some agonize over the decision to retreat? Is money an issue? Time? Or, is it fear? Let me assure you there is no need to put off an opportunity to improve your spiritual life. You may not feel desperate, but are you starving for serenity, needing rest in the solitude, a willingness to embrace new possibilities, or to strengthen your relationship with God?

I understand that money is tight for many people. Let's be honest; we waste a lot of money on things of little importance, way less important than improving our spiritual condition. Put aside a jar somewhere in your home. Label it: *My Lifesaver, or Retreat Funds, or Sanity Jar*. Begin throwing spare change into it. Rather than a six-dollar coffee, make a cup at home, and put the money in your jar. Save for one year and treat yourself to a retreat weekend. Most retreat centers offer scholarships to help defray the costs of retreats. Don't let money be your excuse for missing out on a retreat experience.

Make time for yourself. Carve out one weekend a year just for you and God to meet in a very special setting. There are thousands of retreat centers across the United States and abroad. With the internet, you can explore many possibilities, and find something that feels inviting, filled with warm embraces, lots of wisdom, peace and quiet, and natural beauty. Look for a place where you can slow down and really feel and hear God speaking to you. Retreat to the ocean, to the mountains, or to a center tucked into the woods and off the beaten path. Maybe the city is inviting to you. There are group and themed retreats, silent retreats, guided and directed retreats available. Length of stay varies depending on the retreat. People will give you space, listen to what you need to say, and encourage you at every opportunity.

Is fear holding you back? Are you imagining being on your knees in prayer, eating only bread and water all weekend? Do you imagine only holier-than-thou types of people attending this experience? Do you feel like you have secret places inside of you that others may want you to reveal? Is it difficult for you to come together with other people you do not know? Does a quiet, uncomplicated, and serene place feel unnerving, compared to your busy lifestyle?

*Ponder:* Retreating is no doubt a risk. Your life will change. You will not be the same person you were upon entering the retreat setting. Whatever the joys, challenges, or disappointments may be in your life, be reassured others will be there to journey with you. No one is walking around with halos. You will feel infused by a spirit of love and companionship. Your desire to remain connected to God will grow. You will find yourself renewed and willing to serve others with a new attitude. Gratitude will permeate your being. Stillness will replace frenetic doing. You will begin to explore the endless possibilities that God has in store for you!

There is a retreat house waiting for you when you are ready. Do an internet search, call, email, ask a friend, or talk to your clergy. Take the risk. You will be changed.

**Prayer:** Dear God, teach me how to abandon myself to you in quiet places both within and outside of myself. Let me respond to your call to stop continually doing and find time for being. May I appreciate the Sabbath time you encourage.

*Ezekiel 20:12*
*Psalm 39: 2-5*
*Galatians 5:25*

# Accepting Prayers

*"As it turns out, if one person is praying for you, buckle up. Things can happen."*
Anne Lamott

***Pause and Reflect:*** I needed help from others to complete a book I was writing during the summer. Not only did others volunteer their input, I received prayers for inspiration. I'd been asking for ideas and participation when it came to putting together my religious education programs for the fall. Parents and members of my church stepped forward to offer assistance. Many told me they were praying for the success of the program. My watercolor painting had become dry and uninspired. Friends shared ideas and sent creative energy my way. I was challenged by negative thoughts around a relationship and people were there to offer wisdom and prayers.

We all need to learn to ask for help. We may have heard things as we were growing up, like: "you'll figure it out on your own," "pull yourself up by your bootstraps," "if you want it done right, do it yourself." That's all well and good, when that is possible. We all come to a time or place in our lives when that just doesn't work as well as if we ask for help. We need others to inspire us, share their ideas, or pitch in and work with us. From simple requests that ease our load, to more important help that changes the direction of our lives, everyone needs reassurance, direction, or inspiration at times. Asking for help can be a prayer. We become willing to relinquish control and accept a gift presented to us, in whatever forms it is given.

When we receive a gift from another person, whether it is their time, attention, talent, encouragement or prayers, it's important for us to express our gratitude. A simple "thank you" is the thing that makes our heart sing and feel joyful! But expressing gratitude is more than simply saying "thank you." Gratitude is a state of being filled with love. When our hearts are filled with appreciation, we feel warmth and light. It is in that fullness that we then are able to more fully give back to others. It's as if we become bearers of light to others.

When someone in our life takes the time to do something to help make us feel more at ease, our hearts overflow. When God graces us with the willingness to let go of control and we discover new ways to approach problems and concerns, we are enlightened. When we discover new doors opening and we're willing to walk through them, we experience courage. Simply asking someone to keep us in their prayers offers unforeseen possibilities.

***Ponder:*** By delegating tasks, inviting others to help out, and sharing responsibilities, we can find ourselves saying, "wow, I'm so blessed to have these people in my life." We find that our anxieties can be quelled by asking for what we need. By sharing our desires with others, we often ignite a spark in others' creativity. We find that God is doing for us what we can't do alone. Remember, God often appears with skin on. The simple kindnesses we experience from others are a reason for a grateful heart. As we begin to pay attention and notice the wonderful gifts we receive in the course of our day, it's cause for joyful celebration. Graciously accept the prayers and good intentions of others. Sit back and watch in amazement how your life can be transformed.

***Pray:*** Dear God, my heart sings at the generous spirit of others. Help me to graciously accept the positive intentions of those you have placed along my journey to help guide, inspire, and pray for me.

*Acts 12:5*
*Colossians 4:2*
*Romans 12:12*

# The Path Of Faith

*"No single decision you ever made*
*has led in a straight line to*
*where you find yourself now."*
Deepak Chopra

**Pause and Reflect:** The path has always been a strong metaphor for the journey of our life. Bends, twists, and forks represent the choices we must make along the way.

In his poem, *The Road Less Travelled*, author Robert Frost describes the traveler coming to a fork in the road and looking down both paths. The journeyman must choose one. It isn't that one path is necessarily better than the other, since both paths seem equally worn. Unless he wants to stand there all day, the traveler must choose one.

There are many times we, too, are faced with a choice. We are free to choose whichever path we wish to take. Sometimes, we make a choice based on our intellectual knowledge or past experiences. We may trust our intuition in making a decision. Still, other times, we must take a risk, a chance.

By practicing sound spiritual principles in our daily life, we can be assured of choosing a path while knowing that God is with us. It's true we don't have the gift of hindsight when making choices. Risk is inherent in many choices. But who better to take a risk with than God.

Many of us spend too much time being indecisive and fearful when it comes to decisions. "Is it the best choice?" "What will others say?" "What will it mean for my future?" "Is it too risky?" How many times have you, like me, procrastinated with a decision rather than just made one? Today, we can trust our gut instincts and make the best choice possible. Why? Because once we've asked God to help us, we receive help through our intuitions, the Holy Spirit, intellect, and experiences. God is present in it all.

If, down the road, we find out that because of circumstances, the decision we made no longer serves God and others, we are free to take another path. As a result we no longer need to waste time and energy on regretting past choices. The choices we've made have served to teach us valuable lessons about what's important in life. Rather than looking back on what could have been, we can make a choice to live in, *what is right before us*.

***Ponder:*** Scripture says, "We live by faith and not by sight." 2 Corinthians 5:7 We are not alone. We have many companions who choose to live in God's light. To live a meaningful life means to be fully engaged in living out the gospel. We imitate the examples of Christ, and center our lives in him. We trust God to guide our path. There is no need to worry about the future because God is our constant companion on the journey. While our senses help us to navigate the physical world it is our faith that guides us along a path of much greater joy and peace. We cannot see God with the human eye, but we can experience God in our lives.

***Pray:*** Dear God, help me to walk by faith. May I trust you to lead me wherever it is I must go. Give me the strength and courage to remain steadfast in my faithfulness to doing your will.

*Hebrews 11:1*
*Deuteronomy 7:9*
*1 Corinthians 10:13*

# The Second Half

*" The first half of my life I went to school,*
*the second half of my life I got an education."*
Mark Twain

**Pause and Reflect:** For those of us riding the waves into the second half of our lives, we're making new discoveries about ourselves that help us to access a deeper wisdom, beauty, and love.

I sat in a weekend workshop learning more about my personality type and how I experience the reality of the world around me and in me. There are many theories and tools used for helping us to notice our behaviors, what motivates us, and where our passions lie. Over the years I've been exposed to the MBTI, Four Temperaments, Enneagram, Strength Finder, and even a personality test based on colors. It's a billion dollar industry these days, and while I always have a healthy skepticism about labels, I must admit there is value in looking closely at what makes us tick.

Admittedly, hearing characteristics of my type were not easy to sit with. I'm described as over-efficient, over-programmed, too much energy in outer image vs. inner image, product more important than people, self doubt, and approval needed for performance and achievement. Years ago, I may have focused only on the negative.

This time, throughout the workshop, I was reminded of my transformation and conversion over the years, a time in my life where I can see both beauty and brokenness. Today, I'm aware of the potential pitfalls when my vanity grows larger than my dependence on God, when I fail to slow down and take time for playing, when I have lofty expectations of others and myself, or when I do not risk for fear of failure.

As I continue to place God at the center of my life I'm getting in touch with the person God intends for me to be. Less time is spent trying to be what I think others want me to be. I'm finding my true self. Rather than comparing myself with others, I find myself trying to understand what it's like walking in their shoes. I'm trusting that things will get done without me. My way is not the only way! Most of all, I am learning to embrace whatever is happening in the moment no matter how it feels. Feelings are fleeting; they will pass and take a new shape. Nothing is so important that my inner peace should be disturbed. God is in the discomfort and the joy. When I trust God with my whole self, I find serenity.

*Ponder:* Do we fail to always make these connections? YES!!!! Today, we can embrace our imperfections.

We are not simply a number, a category, a set of letters or definitions. Certainly, we come to learn about ourselves through life experiences. Our conversion will be one of deepening faith in God, in love and truth. No longer afraid to know our truest self, we will experience a freedom beyond all understanding. This is what happens to the seasoned man and woman. The people of wisdom are no longer chained to old habits of reacting to life; rather they find joy in embracing its fullness. Cheers to the second half!

*Pray:* Dear God, help me to continue my conversion of mind and heart so that it always reflects you. May I always remain flexible and teachable.

*James 3:13*
*Proverbs 19:8*
*Romans 14:5*

# October

# Beauty and Brokenness

*"Soul is not a thing,*
*but a quality or a dimension of*
*experiencing life and ourselves.*
*It has to do with depth, value, relatedness,*
*heart, and personal substance."*
Thomas Moore

***Pause and Reflect:*** So just how do we take the very ordinary, mundane happenings of everyday life and see in them the depth and breadth of God? We learn to live into them, experience them. We must feel them with our bodies, see them with our heart, listen to them with sacred ears, savor them with a clean palate, and intuit them with a deep sense of attention.

A few recent experiences that have led me to touch in to soulful experiences:

Having lived in my present home for several years, it was only very recently that I discovered a beautiful path in the woods around a reservoir a quarter mile from my house. Taking early morning jogs in this serene and beautiful place has stirred my soul. I find myself anticipating the sunrise so I can set off into the woods. I hear the geese and birds sing morning songs of praise. My eyes take in the beautiful color as the trees change into autumn dress. The smells of fallen leaves and pine needles permeate the fresh, crisp morning air. My body relaxes, stretches, and moves to a gentle rhythm much different than the excess rigor of past exercise. Thank you, God, for this place of stillness.

My heart fills with gratitude knowing that my life's work is something I love. I had an opportunity to facilitate a retreat weekend on the Maine coast. It did not escape me that many had come to rest and renew their spirit. The first evening of retreat I asked everyone to simply notice how beauty and brokenness played a role in their lives. Many stories of brokenness and beauty unfolded over the weekend. My soul was filled with a wealth of wisdom. One woman in particular grabbed my heartstrings. In her twilight years, she described feelings of inadequacy and fear of death. She was failing to see the gifts she brings to others in the present. I will not forget her gentle, humble spirit. Thank you, God, for wisdom offered in our brokenness and seasoned years.

I received a call from a friend who needed a listening ear. To be present to, and hold her questions, discomfort, and uneasy emotions, was a gift to my soul. Thank you, God, for the reminder that we are not islands unto ourselves. We need one another.

While on retreat a song was sung to open the Mass. The melody was beautiful, but a word caught my attention deep within. Freedom. As I gazed out the window I saw an American flag waving in the brisk wind. I could no longer sing as my body was choked with gratitude. I could barely keep down the tears. How blessed we are to live in a land where we have the freedoms that give us the opportunity to nourish our souls. Thank you God, for your bounty. May it be our reminder to serve others in need and continually appreciate our daily gifts.

I learned about a young man, who, because of illness, has suffered a great deal on his life's journey. His mom shared that he rarely complains about the pain, taking his medication, or frequent doctor visits and hospitalizations. An opportunity arose to be a conduit to helping him fulfill a lifetime dream. My daughter-in-law provided the necessary connections. My heart was smiling from ear to ear after receiving a text from his mother saying he was having the time of his life. Thank you, God, for opportunities to lighten the load of someone who needs their spirits lifted.

***Ponder:*** Brokenness and beauty often seems a double-edged sword. We have opportunities to experience the gifts of both, every day. We may respond to our life circumstances by running away or being present to them. How do you see God in the depth, value, relatedness, heart, and personal substance of your daily experiences?

***Pray:*** Dear God, teach us how to be present to encounters of the soul. May we learn to appreciate the lessons of both beauty and brokenness in our daily lives.

*Psalm 46:1-3*
*2 Corinthians 12: 9-10*
*Hebrews 4:15-16*

# Family

*"This is the nest in which soul is born,
nurtured, and released into life."*
Thomas Moore

*Pause and Reflect:* Nowhere do we have more soulful experiences than in our families. Family experiences are as real as it gets. Drama, suffering, silliness, sheer joy, and madness are part of the family dynamics. Over the course of our lifetimes we get to know family members inside and out. We see their human nature, gifts, idiosyncrasies, and flaws. We can love someone in our family and still shake our heads in disbelief at their choices and actions.

We like to throw out the word *dysfunctional* to describe some families, but honestly, isn't every family familiar with chaos and discord? Celebrations and crises bring us together and break us apart. There are members of our family that we'd probably never associate with except for the fact that they are family!

Families provide a melting pot of memories that reach deep into our felt senses and stay with us for a lifetime. In caring for our soul, we don't try to fix what feels bad, and restore what we may imagine was blissful; rather we take the raw, down-to-earth reality of what is, and let that become our teacher. We learn to appreciate the gifts that emerge in both the muck and the wisdom of our families.

Moore writes in *Care of the Soul*, "It takes extreme diligence and concentration to think differently about the family: to appreciate its shadow as well as its virtue and simply to allow stories to be told without slipping into interpretations, analysis, and conclusions."

It's not always easy to do, but God calls us to compassion, understanding, and forgiveness. It's easy to want to run from the shadows and pretend they do not exist. We can run, but we can't escape the very fabric into which we've been woven. We can honor the soul by making peace with our stories. Then, we are free to allow the Spirit to form new stories within us. What emerges has the potential to help us grow emotionally and spiritually into the person God intends us to be.

***Ponder:*** Soul-discovery embraces and celebrates the family. Whether we are still in the nest, have left it, or are in the process of forming our own new nest, let us honor the past and present, the cast of characters, and memories that are a part of the very fabric of who we are. How have we learned to appreciate both the shadows and goodness in our families? Why is it important for me to recognize both?

***Pray:*** Dear God, thank you for my ancestors on whose shoulders I've stood, my family of origin who have loved me unconditionally, and for the gifts of our current family, immediate and extended. May this tapestry of your love unfold for generations to come.

*Psalm 103:17-18*
*Galatians 3:28*
*Romans 12:5*

# Get Over Yourself

*"There are ultimately only two possible adjustments to life;*
*one is to suit our lives to principles; the other is to suit principles*
*to our lives.*
*If we do not live as we think, we soon begin to think as we live.*
*The method of adjusting moral principle to the way men live*
*is just a perversion of the order of things."*
Fulton J. Sheen

***Pause and Reflect:*** If you're like me, you occasionally have those days when you have to say, "You just need to get over yourself"- to yourself! Those days when you think your opinions are the only ones that matter. Times when the pity pot you're sitting on has outlived its usefulness.

Perhaps there are days when whatever is happening isn't happening fast enough, or when attention is drifting toward others, and you want more of the limelight.

Self-absorption is a human condition that demands our attention. We need to replace self-absorption with God-absorption.

When we are God-absorbed, self-absorption is replaced by self-love. Be careful not to confuse self-love with being selfish. Loving ourselves is a requirement for living a healthy spiritual life. It is our great *thank you* to God for the many gifts we receive. Loving ourselves comes from a place of humility. We are clear about the difference between the Creator and the created. Self-love allows our inner light to shine outwardly into the world because we know it is of God. A person who loves him or herself accepts and embraces both their shortcomings and gifts.

We must focus ourselves on the very important things of life, not necessarily the serious things of life. When God is at the center of our daily activities, everything that moves outwardly is of love. Living life well frees us of our attachments to self, of being self-absorbed.

Sometimes it's the small attachments that get our attention. My high school reunion was quickly approaching. On one particular day, I was becoming self-absorbed with my wardrobe, and all things *me*. What to wear? Do I shop for a new outfit? How will I wear my hair, up or down? What color nail polish? On and on it went, until finally, with my heart centered in the right place, I thought about what it really meant to be reunited with these friends after thirty-five years. It was OK to want to look my best. It was not OK to be so self-absorbed that I lose sight of what's important.

I went to my reunion to honor relationships and memories from the past. I opened my heart and listened to the present stories and experiences of those with whom I had a connection many years ago. That's the important stuff. It was an evening filled with warm hugs and wonderful stories. I found it less important to know what people were doing, so much as who they were becoming.

**Ponder:** Once in a while we all need reminders to get over ourselves. Self-love helps us to detach from the nonsense and focus on the gifts right in front of us. When was your last visit to the pity-pot? When did you become frustrated that things weren't going as planned, or happening fast enough for you? Looking back, how did you feel and act in your self-absorption? What practices help you move into a place of self-love and acceptance? How does centering your life in God compare to a life centered in self?

**Pray:** Dear God, help me today to suit my life toward living out the gospel message of love toward others and myself. Remove all self-centeredness so that I am open to your will for me.

*Mark 12:31*
*Philippians 2:3-4*
*1 Corinthians 13:4-7*

# A Restless Heart

*"Our heart is restless until it rests in You."*
St. Augustine

***Pause and Reflect:*** Perhaps you've been experiencing the stirrings. Questions keep coming up and feel unresolved. You want answers that don't seem to come. You seem to be questioning other people's desires for you rather than living out your own. There seems to be a lot of outward drama and very little inward peace. You've got lots of ideas and you wonder where to take them. The thought that there has to be more to life keeps popping into your head. You're ready and willing, if you could only figure out the what for.

These may be signs of a restless heart.

Consider a change of perspective. Rather than focusing on the uncomfortable feelings, remind yourself that those feelings are the beginning of something new and wonderful in your life. Those feelings may hold the key to unlocking a new path for you. Stirrings, although they may cause some inner discontent, may be God's way of asking you to pay attention to something new unfolding.

Our new perspective requires trust. When we learn to embrace and surrender our stirrings to God, we are restored to calm. Placing God at the center of our lives creates harmony and balance between action and stillness. It doesn't mean all is resolved and questions are answered. Rather, you are resolved to accepting where you are in the process. You are willing to let go of your expectations and open yourself up for the Spirit to move you in the direction of new possibilities.

It begins with conversation, prayer, meditation, or contemplation. Simply begin to talk with God about your desires. You may want to express them outwardly to someone you trust or write out your thoughts, desires, and ideas. Continue to pray and ask for release from any jumbled thoughts. Ask God to help you focus on the important matters of your soul. Rest in God and be assured that your intuition, your gut instincts, the pull of your heartstrings, and your intellect speak a language you will understand.

***Ponder:*** A restless heart may be God's way of announcing changes. Pay attention to your true desires. Be patient. Open yourself to the possibilities. The next time you're feeling restless, take some time to be still. Take an elevator from your head into the core of your body. Ask yourself, "What is stirring within me?" Take as much time as you need to listen. Rather than having expectations or trying to figure it out, just pay attention to what is revealed.

***Pray:*** Dear God, Help me to understand that you indeed are present in my restlessness. May I be present to it and look for signs of what might need to be let go, or welcomed into my life.

*Psalm 6:2-6*
*Isaiah 38:13-14*
*Job 3:17*

# The Whole Picture

*" My after-forty face felt far more comfortable*
*than anything I lived with previously.*
*Self-confidence was a powerful beauty-potion;*
*I looked better because I felt better.*
*Failure and grief as well as success and love*
*had served me well. Finally, I was tapping into*
*that most hard-won of youth dews: Wisdom."*
Nancy Collins

***Pause and Reflect:*** Please don't mistake this reflection for an ego trip. I assure you, it was rather a moment of insight into the after-fifty me.

My first book, *Ordinary Awakenings,* had its final edit and was ready for publishing. Along with the manuscript, my publisher asked me to bring along a picture for the book cover. I had procrastinated for several months and it was now crunch time. My son, who is great with the camera, was home for a short visit, so I thought it would be a great opportunity to get the picture taken.

I had come home after a long day at work, feeling exhausted. My son informed me that we had about twenty minutes of good daylight to get a picture taken. Reluctantly, I threw a scarf around my neck and went outside to pose for pictures.

I'm not kidding when I say that a hundred pictures later - and feeling a little silly doing this photo shoot - we seemed to find one picture that resonated with the judges: my son, husband, and myself.

Only a few years ago I would never have agreed to take a picture without make-up, without taking a fresh shower and blow-drying my hair, or without changing into an appropriate outfit. I hadn't even put a comb through my hair!

It was important to me that this picture reflects the person I feel I've grown into today. The young girl who was haunted by the camera for many years, the young woman who thought she had to look and act a certain way to please others, the aging woman afraid of wrinkles, has come a long way.

When I looked at the picture, I was able to embrace the lines and wrinkles. I saw past the lack of make-up and disheveled hair thrown up in a ponytail. What I saw was a woman who feels at peace with her life, a seasoned woman who understands the struggles and appreciates the moments of joy. I see a woman who knows the loud, negative voices in her head, but revels in the quiet whispers deep within her body. As I looked upon this photo, I saw serenity on my face, my upward glance giving gratitude to God for the many blessings in my life. This is a woman who is becoming her authentic self and is willing to take a risk when she feels the movement of the Spirit inside of her.

***Ponder:*** There is a difference between knowing that beauty is an inside job, and feeling it resonate in one's heart. That is the work of God. I cannot say this enough: when God becomes the center of our life we begin to recognize the beams of light radiating within us. We want them to shine from within us and out into the world.

Find a picture that captures who you really feel you are. What is it that you see within yourself that resonates outwardly to the world? How do you feel as you look at the picture? Is there a connection with the loving and beautiful spirit within you and the Divine?

Amen for the time and experiences that soften us with the grace of wisdom.

***Pray:*** Dear God, may we fall in love with the amazing possibilities within our minds and bodies. May the frivolous things that hold us back from experiencing true beauty be let go of and replaced with wisdom.

*1 Peter 3:4*
*1 Samuel 16:7*
*Song of Solomon 4:7*

# Surround Us

*"Father,...Open our eyes to see that you are all things,*
*the light and the darkness,*
*not only those things that seem good in our eyes,*
*but horrifyingly unexplainable.*
*Wrap us up inside of the cloud and reveal the mysteries*
*that can only be learned in places of sorrow,*
*that when we walk out we will be like Moses,*
*transformed by the shadow and beaming*
*with the radiant light of your glory.*
*Give us the strength to love on,*
*though our hearts are broken."*
Anna White

***Pause and Reflect:*** Surround us with the light of Your Presence.

Surround us with people who come into our life with a genuine heart. It matters not whether they have shortcomings, so long as they can learn to own them. We don't need smiles that hide disingenuous dispositions; instead let them speak their truths.

Surround us with people who respond to humor and a little self-deprecation, who don't take themselves too seriously. Surround us with those who enlighten us with wisdom that originates from the Holy Source. Those who dance, sing, and speak with joy and wonderment.

Surround us with seekers. Those who think outside the box. People who delight in the simple gifts the universe has to offer. Surround us with the ones who love creativity.

Surround us with leaders who shun arrogance and self-adulation and who care only to serve others as their mission. Gift us with true warriors, those who persevere in the face of injustice, illness, grief and sorrow.

Surround us with a holy and nurturing darkness. Help us to understand its purpose.

Place the *listeners* in our path. The ones who welcome us just as we are. The patient journeymen and women willing to travel uncomfortable roads with us.

Surround us with the ones you need us to love despite our own unwillingness at times. Help us to see you in them.

Surround us with many languages, but let the only one that really matters be love.

Surround us with silence, if only for a while, that we can pause, breathe, and take you in.

And when we feel surrounded by suffering and sadness, anger and resentment, evil and emptiness, wrap your loving arms around us, reminding us of your grace-filled and loving presence.

**Ponder:** Transformation happens in both joyful and painful experiences. Think about the times in your life when change has come as the result of great happiness. When has your life been transformed after great sorrow? How was God revealed to you along the journey? Sometimes it's easier for us to find God in happy times. We can look back in scripture and see how our ancestors, though struggling and feeling alone, were resolved to put their faith in a Mysterious and Loving God.

**Pray:** Dear God, surround me with your presence. No matter what my circumstances are in this moment, help me to trust that you are by my side through it all.

*Joshua 1:9*
*Genesis 28:15*
*Exodus 33:14*

# Blessed Are We

*"May you feel life as an irresistible invitation*
*to discover and develop your talents,*
*each day bringing something new to birth."*
John O'Donohue

***Pause and Reflect:*** Last week was a full one! Back-to-back retreats with participants that share a common bond of faith. It's simply amazing to watch retreat groups, most of whom do not know one another, come together over the course of a few days to find support on a much deeper level than they may have thought possible.

It happens over and over again, and yet, it still feels exciting and new with every group encounter. For those of you, women or men, who have not been on a retreat in many years, or for those who have never experienced retreat, it may be time to seriously consider attending one.

Perhaps the idea of retreat conjures up images of long hours of reciting prayers on your knees, theological lectures that go right over your head, fasting, old buildings with musty smelling chapels, church music that sounds like a funeral dirge, and grandmotherly types with halos practically floating above their heads! Nothing could be further from that reality.

While prayer and meditation is encouraged, you may be surprised to find that it is practiced in many forms. For example, Centering prayer, Lectio Divina, and Focusing, although steeped in tradition, are practiced with a more contemporary flare. The program talks are timely and down-to-earth. All have the opportunity to share in small group discussions. If sharing seems overwhelming, then listening is perfectly acceptable. Participants are encouraged to listen deep down inside to where God is calling. Some seek quiet, some rest, and yet others a contemplative period of retreat. Music and movement, nature and stillness are most often part of the experience. Spiritual companioning and discussions often open windows to the soul.

Retreat participants are supportive and accepting. Many have walked a similar journey with joys and trials. The chapels are bright and airy, peaceful and inviting. You will find yourself desiring more and more quiet time with the Holy One. The music is a mixture of familiar and new. You are encouraged to drift in a wave of serenity.

The hospitality is amazing, and chances are you will not want to leave when it's time to go. At the very least you'll be checking the calendar for the next program offering. In my experience, these welcoming places, where strangers find rest, are like being in a home away from home.

Lastly, if you're looking for saints, guess what? You'll find them! All of them will have tarnished halos. We've all had our share of life's difficult moments, but, so, too, we've found our refuge in God. We've journeyed with courage and grace and looked into a future where we can trust the movements of the Holy Spirit. And we do it, knowing we are never alone. Let the people of faith share their hope with you.

***Ponder:*** At one time or another all of us feel restless, overwhelmed, too busy, depleted and exhausted. Perhaps your well has run dry and you are feeling stumped about how to replenish it. Your excuses may sound old and worn out. Maybe it's time to recharge the drained batteries! Don't wait until someday. Today is that day. You deserve to take some time out of your schedule to get filled up.

Does this sound selfish? It is Jesus who teaches us the value of rest and renewal. We can be better spouses, parents, co-workers, and servants of our God, as well as stewards of the earth and ourselves when we take time to get spiritually fit.

I've been retreating for over thirty years and there has never once been a retreat I attended that didn't give me something of spiritual value. Put away the fear, preconceived notions, and excuses. It's *your* time.

There are weekend retreats happening all over the world. Simply enter retreat centers in your area into Google and look for descriptions that seem to suit your needs. Call or find online information describing the place and its offerings. "Amazing," is the word I hear most often, followed by, "*I will be back!*" I encourage husbands or wives to give your spouse the "gift" of a retreat. Any occasion will do. Do whatever it takes to gift yourself.

Retreats aren't to "get spiritual" …you are spiritual! Your body, mind, and spirit are craving the movement of the Holy Spirit. Go. Let every sense come alive in you.

***Pray:*** Dear God, lead me to you! Help me to take some much-needed time for personal reflection and prayer. Let my retreat time be an opportunity for rest and renewal. Holy Spirit, lead me toward action rather than inaction.

*Isaiah 30:15*
*Psalm 39:2-5*
*Luke 5:16*

# November

# Wisdom Is A Precious Jewel

*"When you look to your future,*
*you see yourself alone, old, and foolish.*
*These thoughts are demons, nothing more.*
*You are lovable. Even as we speak, you are greatly beloved.*
*I cherish you. To me you are more valuable than*
*diamonds, emeralds, sapphires or rubies.*
*You are my great treasure, the pearl beyond price."*
Julia Cameron

***Pause and Reflect:*** We recently lost the feminine matriarch of our family at the age of ninety-seven. My Auntie Julie was truly one of those women who was in many ways ahead of her time. Independent and open to possibilities, she left home and traveled for work and fun when most women in her day stayed close to home. She married a divorcee when she was in her forties, which was seen by some outside the family as scandalous. She started a family later in life. Her wit and humor were infectious. Devotion to faith and family was a priority. God remained at the center of her life. Although her husband died more than twenty- five years prior, she surrounded herself with family and friends. If she felt the demon of aloneness at times, she never let on. In her obituary it was said, "she was still learning to be old." I believe her heart and spirit were as free as a young child.

As a family, we cherished her as a gift. Her wisdom and strength have taught each of us to courageously face our seasoned aging with grace and deep faith in God.

So the question I ponder as I look upon a life well-lived is, "What do I cherish more than any earthly treasure?"

Preparing for a recent presentation I found my answer in scripture. These words gave meaning and validation to my thoughts. "For God loves nothing so much as the person who dwells with Wisdom…" Wisdom 7:28

Wisdom, personified in sacred scripture in the feminine, is a gift from the

Holy Spirit. She doesn't make life easy. She doesn't make me right all the time. She doesn't help me foretell the future. Wisdom does not know boundaries such as intelligence, age, physicality, religiosity, or social status. So, what is this jewel that scripture reminds us, "comes from the Lord?"

Life experiences are rich with wisdom. It's not necessarily what I know in my life that makes a difference so much as what I'm open to learning. I've fallen into very narrow chasms throughout my life. Places that seem to smother the light. There have been times when all I saw when I looked up was a mere dot of light. That small dot of light represented hope. Wisdom isn't always recognized or understood when we're in the chasms of life. It's the lifelines that are thrown to us while were in the chasm that make a difference. Do we cling to them? Are we willing to use them to help us move toward the light? Are we grateful for the lifeline? Do we trust God enough to hang on through the difficult climb upward? Can we use those lifelines to aid others in need?

To dwell in Wisdom is to trust God to continue forming us into the authentic person we are meant to be. As the Serenity Prayer suggests we need to come to terms with the things we cannot change, understand when we can make changes, and ultimately pray for the gift of wisdom to help us discern the difference between the two.

***Ponder:*** Pause is what we need. When we have a question about something, when we are frustrated or confused or when we are struggling with an issue we must pause and consciously invite God into our discernment. It is the gift of Wisdom from the Holy Spirit that enlightens us. And our enlightenment comes not on our timetable but on God's. Often, the most difficult part of Wisdom is waiting on her: sitting patiently with the not-yet-answered and accepting the what-is-here-and-now!

We often joke between me and my sisters that I'm the Auntie Julie (matriarch) of our family. I'm the oldest of seven children. Oh, that God will grant me the wisdom to ripen each day of my life, as did my mom's oldest sister, opening myself up to God's will. To speak up if necessary, to shut up when necessary, to wait patiently for answers and above all to accept and give thanks for all that presently *is*. I don't always do this well, but it is what I strive to do each day. My Auntie had the knack for living in the present moment. Wisdom certainly found her jewel in Julie.

How has wisdom shown herself on your journey? Is there anything that blocks you from receiving wisdom as a precious jewel? What gifts have emerged through wisdom?

***Pray:*** Dear God, give us the wisdom to patiently wait on you and to be with whatever is present to us in the moment.

*Colossians 2:2-3*
*Proverbs 16:16*
*Job 12:12*

# Leave It To The Kids

*"You will find more happiness growing down than up."*
Author Unknown

**Pause and Reflect:** It was the first annual Pumpkin Festival, and I was organizer- in-chief. My children have grown up, and I was a little anxious about the activities I was planning for other children. Would the older kids find it boring? Was there enough to keep them all busy? Was this event over-planned or under-planned? Would moms and dads step up, and show up? Would the prayer service be too long? As I've shared with my readers previously, part of my nature is an underlying anxiety about pretty much everything! However, I'm finding ways to be present with it, rather than ignore it.

As I drove to the parish center at eight o'clock in the morning to set up for the late afternoon event, I prayed, "Dear God, give me patience, help me to slow down and enjoy the activity of this day, help me to take a few breaths, and if things feel a little crazy inside, remind me of your presence." During the preparations, every time a question surfaced inside of me, I paused, took a breath, and reminded myself that God was present, and that all shall be well.

As everyone was arriving and the activities began, I took my cue from the children. By giving them something to focus on, like carving a pumpkin, they became riveted with creativity. They enjoyed working side by side with their peers and the adults. They helped one another to complete the task. Their joy was evident as they displayed their creations. We had smiling pumpkins, pumpkins with ears, and pumpkins with every kind of nose possible. Add a box of Crayolas, rocks and paint, beanbags to toss, a bowling game made from plastic soda bottles and paint, and a cupcake walk, and these kids were smiling and laughing and creating and having fun.

Sometimes in this technical world we forget that simple things, done together with those you trust and love, grow our capacity for happiness. My heart was overflowing as parents and children gathered for our prayer service. Pumpkins of all shapes, sizes and colors lighted the room as we recalled that God had picked us as part of his creation. We were reminded it is God who gets inside our hearts and minds and scoops out all the seeds of doubt, greed, and unkindness. And then, it is God who lets his light shine inside of us for the entire world to see. It was truly magical watching all the children sing and pray and play together along with their families.

As I shut down the lights and stepped into the dark, cool night, Jesus' words came to mind, " Truly I tell you, unless you change and become like little children you will never enter the Kingdom of heaven." Matt. 18:3

***Ponder:*** So just how do we *grow down*, so as to gain a little bit of heaven each day?

Get a box of crayons and color.
Walk in the rain.
Take an afternoon cookie break.
Sit under a tree and read.
Rake a pile of leaves and take a gentle jump in.
Carve a pumpkin.
Play Red Rover or Hide and Seek with children.
Chase butterflies.
Pray *simply,* and on your knees with your hands folded.
Wear something bright or mismatched.
Don't wear make-up, for a change.
Pick flowers.
Make a card and send it to a friend.

Take a cue from your children, grandchildren, or neighborhood kids. Join in their simple fun. Ask God to open your heart and mind to become child-like in spirit. See what happens when you *grow down*?

***Pray:*** Dear God, help me to seek the child within me yearning for joy, peace, creativity, hope, and love. May I never grow up so much that I lose sight of the simple pleasures in life.

*Matthew 19:14*
*1 Peter 2:2*
*Psalm 71: 5-6*

# A New Story Is Emerging

*"The gospel writer goes to great pains to set the scene*
*and to indicate all that Jesus is aware of*
*as he gets ready to wash the feet of his disciples.*
*Judas Iscariot is among them, his heart ready to betray Jesus.*
*Jesus knows that Peter will deny him*
*and that others will run away.*
*Imagine yourself there as Jesus goes around the table.*
*How do you react when Jesus comes to your feet?*
*What do you want to say to him?"*

William A. Barry, S.J.

***Pause and Reflect:*** Imagine yourself as a character in a scripture story. It is often a wonderful jumping off point for prayer and contemplation. After all, it's easy to forget that these characters were real people, with real feelings, just like you and I. By placing ourselves into the story, we have an opportunity to begin to look at our reactions toward Jesus and others. We may formulate questions, and perhaps share our thoughts silently with God. In the quiet of our hearts, we may reflect on what God is trying to communicate to us through an ancient event or story.

This use of imagination allows us to express our desires before God in a very real way. We leave the theology lesson aside and enter the heart of the story, which really becomes the heart of *our* story.

For example, if we were to read the passage from John's gospel that describes Jesus' washing the disciples' feet, we might understand the symbolism of service, humility, and purity. But, let's place ourselves in that room. What do you expect Jesus' demeanor to be, given that he knows his hour has come to pass from earth to heaven? What feelings does this conjure up in you? Is there anything you want to say to Jesus?

When Jesus ties a towel around his waist, pours water into a basin, and begins to wash your feet, what is going on inside of you? Do you feel honored, humbled, afraid, or ashamed? Do you wonder about your response toward serving others, your community, your family, and the environment? What questions might you ask Jesus about his decision to wash his disciples feet? Jesus announces that there is one in the room who will betray him. Do you feel any sadness or remorse? Judas has been labeled the betrayer, but how often are you distracted by power, prestige, self-will, and things of little spiritual value? How does it feel sitting at the table? Do you want to point a finger rather than look deeply at your own shortcomings? Is there anything you want to ask Judas? Do you want to understand more about Jesus' feelings toward Judas?

You are still in the room. Now, aware that he soon will leave them, he gives them a command: "Love each other. Just as I have loved you, you should love each other." Sit quietly and let those words sink in. How do you receive God's love? Do you believe God is crazy about you? Do you trust him in all things? Do you love others only when you feel they deserve it, or do you love as Jesus did, unconditionally? Who in your life is difficult to love? Jesus looks into your eyes. He knows your thoughts, your heavy heart.. What do you want to tell him now?

Later, you are with Peter when he's tormented by Jesus' words: "…before the rooster crows tomorrow morning, you will deny three times that you even know me." What troubles your heart at this moment? Is there stress, grief, anxiety, loss, or lack of peace of mind? Have you turned these things over to God? Do you have faith in God to help you? How often do you fail to let go, deny God's help, and continue to depend on your own willpower to get through life's trials?

*Ponder:* We've heard many of these scripture stories over and over again since childhood. Allow yourself to imagine a new way to come to God in prayer. By placing yourself in the stories, you may be gifted with a new perspective and dialogue that allows your inner story to unfold from the Word.

*Pray:* Dear God, let your Word sink deeply into my heart and awareness, so that new stories may emerge from your ancient wisdom.

*John 4:7-10*
*Mark 5: 25-34*
*John 5: 5-15*

# Put Up Your Sh_t Shield!

*"He will cover you with his feathers,*
*and under his wings you will find refuge;*
*his faithfulness will be your shield and rampart."*
Psalm 91:4

***Pause and Reflect:*** I received some of the best advice, words of wisdom, from a religious sister for whom I have the utmost respect. She shall remain anonymous.

I'd been having some difficulty letting go of a soured relationship. I was at the point where I was feeling little trust, plenty of hurt, and no response to my reaching out to talk things over. A part of me had been resisting, leaving it be. I felt myself wanting to argue my point, or make it right, or give the person the silent treatment. I even resisted being overtly kind because it felt phony.

After venting my feelings with Sister, she admittedly chose a kind of spiritual cliché in response. She asked if I could see Jesus in this person. In other words, could I see the goodness rather than glaring defects? I admitted honestly that while my head knew that was the right approach, my heart was still struggling with it. Did I know there was goodness in this person with whom I was struggling? Yes, of course. Why then, did I resist letting go? I suppose, that like many of us who have experienced these difficulties in a relationship we want what was, what may have been, and it's difficult to accept change.

"Well," Sister said, "there is something else you could do. It was suggested to me at one time." I eagerly awaited her gentle words of wisdom. "You can put up your *sh_t shield*!" I had to laugh. First, it caught me off guard, coming out of her mouth in a moment when I, quite frankly, thought I would hear some uplifting spiritual tidbit.

But, the Holy Spirit works in mysterious ways, and these words were just what I needed.

As the words rolled off her tongue, I appreciated the down-to-earth approach she took to helping me get the message I needed to hear. Some words emphasize a point very well. This particular evening I needed a little humor as well as a visual aid. The *shield* made perfect sense.

She described the cross around her neck, worn as a symbol by her religious community, as her shield. When she places her hand around the cross she is aware of God's protection surrounding her. She went on to describe how others used the metaphor to help them visualize their protective shields.

I visualized a strong barrier of light surrounding my body. It protects me from taking anyone's baggage in, or letting any negativity of my own go out. It is, in fact, a spiritual barrier. The light is God's protection and power present to me. When I visualize Christ's light surrounding me I want to remain in that calmness. Words and actions lose their sting because I don't need to take things personally. Phoniness can't bother me; it's not mine to own. I can accept the hurt without needing to fuel a fire by my own hurtful responses. I can forgive without the need to reconcile. I can let go of another's stuff and just be myself.

Putting up the *shield* for me is about freedom. It's about not taking others or myself too seriously. It reminds me that there is balance between life's comedic and tragic moments. Light-heartedness is crucial. I'm not always going to enjoy the company of some people; however there are so many who bring me joy. I can choose to surround myself with those who delight in life's simple pleasures and pray for those who do not choose light. And it helps me mourn and accept changes in relationships. I'm learning to love differently, unconditionally, and without expectations.

I've been using this metaphor to help me as I process my feelings. It's helping me to rethink my approach with difficult relationships. Just thinking of Sister's words and imagery puts a smile on my face. It's a little edgy, and therefore memorable. And yet, I soften as I think of God's light surrounding me and protecting me from me, and anyone who wishes me harm. Only God's light can do that.

***Ponder:*** What symbol or image helps you to remain free from the negative energy of others? When things get really difficult, how do you keep your inner calm in the turbulence that sometimes exists from the outside world?

What does putting up your shield look like for you?

**Pray:** Dear God, when life presents its trials, with people and circumstances that are difficult to bear, remind me to put on a shield of courage, strength, and perseverance that only you can give me as protection. Help me to hold back my arrows and let any that come my way, bounce off.

*Genesis 15:1*
*Proverbs 30:5*
*Psalm 28:7*

# December

# Love As My Anchor

*"Knowing love or the hope of knowing love
is the anchor that keeps us from falling
into a sea of despair."*
Bell Hooks

***Pause and Reflect:*** Isaiah in the Old Testament speaks to us today just as he did to the people of Judah thousands of years ago. "But God's not finished. He's waiting around to be gracious to you. He's gathering strength to show mercy to you. God takes the time to do everything right- - everything. Those who wait around for him are the lucky ones." Isaiah 30:18

It's easy to turn to false gods for relief from our anxieties. Work, lust, drugs, alcohol, food, excesses of power, prestige, objects, and unhealthy relationships can draw us in. We can get lost in the illusion that going outside ourselves for quick fixes will solve our problems. And make no mistake about it; the reason distractions are appealing to us is that they may give us temporary relief. They may make us feel good momentarily; however, in the end, we'll be disappointed and find ourselves singing the old familiar tune, "Is this all there is?"

When we anchor ourselves in God we accept the truth of our lives and become willing to live in its reality. It's not always going to be easy, but the more we simplify our lives, the better our ability to love and be loved. Trusting in God's plan helps us to expand our capacity for love. We no longer feel the need for excessive control, anxieties are calmed, we find opportunities for prayer and presence, and we are mindful of our needs and the needs of others.

We are given the opportunity each day to examine our lives and open ourselves up to God's light. So what exactly are we to examine? Take a look at your relationships. Are you doing everything possible to unconditionally love those members of your immediate family? Have you remembered friends today, not just the ones you see routinely, but also, the ones you don't always see? Are there steps you could take to repair a friendship that has soured? Are you holding grudges with someone, whether a relative, friend, co-worker, or member of your community? Are you taking care of your physical, emotional, and spiritual needs so as to be the best example for others in your life? Have you done something for those less fortunate than yourself or have you only thought about it? It's time for action! Today is the day for new "love-beginnings." Once you start shining your light out into the world, it feels so good that you want to do it more often.

Nothing you find "out there" will fulfill you quite like the love you experience when your life is anchored in God. That's where true love resides. As parents and grandparents, friends and neighbors, teachers and mentors, it's imperative that we give this gift to our young children. In a world constantly bombarding us with a win-at-all-costs, get what you can get now, bigger is better, more is greater mentality, the false gods are in stiff competition for a young person's attention.

*Ponder:* We cannot mentor young people with words alone; they are too smart for that. If we talk about God, but don't take time to worship, they notice. If we talk about prayer but never quiet ourselves to listen for God's response within us, it's noticeable. If we talk about justice and tolerance, but spew slurs, they notice. If we constantly acquire, but do not give back in time, treasure, and talent, they notice. If we invoke God's name in anger, but refuse to accept his forgiveness and mercy, they notice. If we say "I love you" to our children and fail to be present to them, they notice.

How has love proved to be your anchor? In what ways have you failed to let love anchor you? What changes can be made to help you to be more aware of your capacity to let love grow inside of you?

*Pray:* Dear God, grow my capacity to love you and others not only through word but deed as well. Let me never turn away from the light of your face.

*Hebrews 6:19*
*John 3:16*
*Galatians 5:13*

# Who Do You Say That I Am?

*"For Jesus, there are no countries to be conquered,*
*no ideologies to be imposed, no people to be dominated,*
*there are only children, women and men to be loved."*
Henri Nouwen

***Pause and Reflect:*** For those who are Christian, our answer to that question, "Who do you say that I am?" Matt. 16:15, speaks volumes about how we will move through our lives. How we feel about Jesus just may determine the extent to which we go deeper in our relationship with God, others, and ourselves. Our truth, then, comes about through relationship.

Jesus is our King, Brother, Teacher, Healer, Advocate, and Redeemer sent by the Father to manifest his glory into this world. You might ask, "Didn't this take place over two thousand years ago; how is it relevant to us today?" We need to remind ourselves just how important it is that Jesus continues to enter into our lives so that we may be a light for all those who need us.

Jesus, the King, comes to us in his Divinity, a Power greater than our understanding that is not lorded over us. This King came into the world without any fanfare. He was born into a smelly stable surrounded by animals and those considered lowly in stature, including his parents and the shepherds of the fields. His humble beginnings are a daily reminder of how we are to approach God; simply, honestly and without putting on airs.

Jesus, our Brother, helps us to understand our human frailties. He listens to all our gobble-de-gook and helps us to decide, like a good friend, the next best steps. Like a good brother, he doesn't berate us but rather picks us up when we're feeling down. He reassures us that mistakes can be corrected and helps us to find the wisdom to better discern God's will for us. Even in the uncomfortable moments, he is present and willing to listen, or to carry us through when things get too difficult. Jesus asks us to bring our burdens to him. He wants to walk with us and help lighten our load.

Jesus, our Teacher, often comes when we least expect it. The best teachers let us figure things out for ourselves. If we listen closely we hear the question deep within that helps stir up solutions. It's difficult because sometimes the answers lie right in front of us. We are so busy looking for *our* answer that we neglect *his*. Grace is the gift we receive when we stop trying to fix things and accept what cannot be changed by anyone but God. We'll find ourselves saying, "I had nothing to do with that; it had to have been Providence."

Jesus heals us emotionally, physically and spiritually. Gospel writers share their stories of Jesus' healings. So many with illnesses, blindness, and severe inner disturbances were made whole. While there is symbolism involved in these healings, to believe in anything less than a miracle is to dismiss that, with God, all things are possible. Our bodies crave the strength and power that God can provide. We pray for healing. However, we also pray to accept whatever it is that happens as part of a bigger plan. God can and does comfort us when we are going through tough times.

Jesus advocates for us. He is merciful and forgiving. We are called to be holy. If that term conjures up images of halos and feels a bit overwhelming, add a "w" and another "l". Jesus has a unique plan for you. He wants you to be "wholly" the person you are called to be. Remember, before you were even born he had your name written on the palm of his hand. He will never forget you. He has great plans for you! Jesus knows you will mess up from time to time, some times worse than others; however, he begs you not to live in shame. He calls you close and asks you to seek forgiveness and then to listen to his directions. No person pulls for your *wholly-ness* more than Jesus.

Jesus is our Redeemer. He could have had all the power, prestige, social standing and things this world had to offer if he so chose. He died hanging on a cross, stripped of all attachments to this world. He is our example of how to let go of the things that do not matter as we journey toward salvation. We pray that one day we will have the opportunity to see our King, Brother, Teacher, Healer, and Advocate face to face.

***Ponder:*** Ask yourself the question Jesus posed to his disciples: "Who do you say that I am?" Pay close attention to the responses you hear, feel, and sense in your daily encounters and activities. It's a wonderful way to begin to deepen your prayer experience. Perhaps this invitation will draw you in to a loving relationship with a God who comes in the flesh, and can understand your human frailties and joys.

***Pray:*** Dear God, let me get closer to you through your Son, Jesus. He knew joy, suffering, fear, helplessness, and dependence upon only one thing, Your will. In Jesus, may I find a friend, mentor, teacher, and healer.

*John 15:15*
*Proverbs 4:20-22*
*Isaiah 9:6*

# Simple Gifts

*"What you are is God's gift to you,
what you become is your gift to God."*
Hans Urs von Balthasar

**Pause and Reflect:** This may not even be true, but from my perspective it certainly seems like gift giving was much simpler when I was a kid. None of our toys and games had cords attached to them. My youngest sister has four preteen children, and I don't envy her Christmas list this year. Electronics and expensive ticket items abound. What happened to the days when Teenage Mutant Ninja Turtle characters were at the top of a child's wish list for Christmas?

Gift giving certainly has gotten more complicated and overwhelming. And, I'm afraid in the busyness of the season, it's easy to lose our joy for creativity, imagination, and interaction. We succumb to the gift card, and come close to letting the impersonal take over. I'm guilty, too.

So this season, let's commit to foregoing the extravagances, and offer the gift of ourselves to one another. Offer our time, talent, presence, and treasure to those with whom we cross paths. And perhaps make an effort to help those for whom our paths may never cross. Take stock of your relationships, and see if there is anything you can do to spruce them up. Is it possible to listen more intently with a compassionate heart? You can offer to spend time preparing a meal or creating a homemade card for a neighbor who may be alone this Christmas. Is there a child who might enjoy driving through a decorated neighborhood to see Christmas lights with you? Is there a person who may benefit from a warm coat, socks, hat, blanket, or mittens? Hand it to them. If you're dining out, perhaps you can surprise a serviceman or woman who happen to be in the same restaurant, and pay their bill.

We certainly can be more creative when it comes to gift giving! One year, wanting to give a special gift to the people who didn't need another thing, I created a "pie of the month" gift for my parents. Every month I brought a homemade pie to my parents' home. It was a gift that lasted throughout the year. One gal I spoke with is creating a *Twenty-Five Days til Christmas* memory book for her parents, filled with beautiful pictures and stories. Another woman shared with me that during the year she goes to tag sales and recreates something new out of old items. She takes a picture of the old item and attaches it to the newly created gift. How creative! There are many ways we can keep the personal gift in Christmas.

***Ponder:*** Ultimately, there is one way to keep this Christmas personal. Come closer to God. Be your unique self. Be the person God has created you to be. When you attend a Christmas party don't put on airs. When you're out shopping, spend within your means. When you're putting up decorations, forget about trying to outdo the neighbors.

We may see God's awesome gifts in the oceans, mountains, seasons, and all of nature. We may feel God's presence in the wind, or through teardrops caused by an emotional response, or while holding a precious child in our arms. We may hear God speaking in a quiet whisper within.

While we may surely acknowledge there is a God in all of this beauty, there is a tendency for us to take it all for granted. And, in times of turmoil we may ask, "Where is God?"

God's response to us was and is purely gift. He sent his only son, Jesus, into the world. This awesome God came to us naked, vulnerable, and wrapped in swaddling clothes. He came into the world in harsh circumstances, and it got worse for him. Jesus the young man understood rejection, ridicule, and suffering. Ultimately, the gift he brought to the world was teaching us how to be in right relationship with God.

Jesus invites us into this relationship every time we pray. He called God, Father. This was not to identify God by gender, but to signify relationship. Good parents or guardians love, support, and guide their children. Children in right relationship with their parents honor that relationship. Jesus gives us a flesh and bones understanding of what it means to be in relationship with God. We have a loving, compassionate, and merciful God who, although Mystery, is quite accessible to us. Like a good parent, God listens and supports all that we strive to do that is good. When we begin taking a path away from God, we are gently nudged by the movement of the Holy Spirit, back onto a holy road of right relationship with God.

**Pray:** Dear God, this season help us shine a light on our relationships. Let the gifts we offer speak of our relationships with one another. Let us be grateful for the gift of mercy and love God has bestowed upon us, as we prepare to welcome the Christ child into our midst, into our hearts. Let us become a gift to you.

*Exodus 33:14*
*Zephaniah 1:7*
*Psalm 73:28*

# A Prayer For The New Year

*"If we rebuke our heart by a calm, mild remonstrance,
with more compassion for it than passion against it
and encourage it to make amendment,
then repentance conceived in this way
will sink far deeper and penetrate more effectually
than fretful, angry, stormy repentance."*
Francis de Sales

**Pause and Reflect:** This new year's, may we vow not to make any resolutions that hold us bound to success and failure by our standards. Rather, help us to search out what it is that you would have us change, create, or improve in our life.

If it is hope you want us to give, let the beams of light you have created within us shine forth wherever there is darkness. Remind us that even in the loneliest of times we are never alone.

When situations arise that are challenging and difficult, help us clear the space in our heart and mind so that we may solely trust in you. Reveal yourself to us in ways that we may understand. With every experience may we grow in understanding of your will for us.

Let us be of service to those you think may benefit from our time, talent, and treasure. May our resounding, "Yes!" to your call bring comfort, joy, and compassion to those you would have us meet.

May we carry a message of love to those who have fallen on difficult times. Help us to embrace you in the sad of heart, spiritless, and hopeless. Let us be reminded that where we see a brother or sister in need...there you are.

Improve our character; after all, you know we could use some polishing! Give us courage to live as you teach us to do. Help us to practice humility; to let go of our petty wants and desires in order that we may become small and you may increase in our life.

Teach us self-discipline. Not the harsh, ego-centered kind; rather the discipline that gives us a positive attitude toward everyone and everything we encounter in our daily rounds.

Continue to teach us the value of perseverance in all things. From working hard to healing broken relationships, let us strive to continue to take steps that benefit people and the world around us.

Guide our footsteps onto spiritual paths. Enlighten my mind, open my heart, and energize my spirit that my journey will be of benefit to those who follow in my footprints. May those steps only lead us to you.

Give us a grateful heart, that in all things, whether they feel good or not, we may find the buried treasure within every experience. May the last words we say each night and the first words we whisper each morning be "Thank You.
"

**Ponder:** Perhaps we can recall this prayer or one of our own creation each morning for one year. Will it make a difference? I tend to think it will and will be more valuable than the hundreds of resolutions we've made over a lifetime that seem to go by the wayside after a week or so. Rather than trying to change, let's make an effort this year to allow God to change and mold us as he sees fit.

**Pray:** Dear God, may the new year be filled with Blessings, Grace, and Prosperity of deep proportions!

*Romans 12:2*
*2 Peter 3:9*
*James 1:17*

Made in the USA
Middletown, DE
01 November 2016